Do Brilliantly

AS English
Language/Literature

Steve Jeffrey

Series Editor: Jayne de Courcy

Published by HarperCollins*Publishers* Limited
77–85 Fulham Palace Road
Hammersmith
London W6 8JB

www.**Collins**Education.com
On-line support for schools and colleges

First published 2002

ISBN 0 00 712606 9

Steve Jeffrey asserts the moral right to be identified as the author of this work.

British Library Cataloguing in Publication Data
A catalogue record for this book is available from the British Library

Edited by Lorimer Poultney
Production by Kathryn Botterill
Cover design by Susi Martin-Taylor
Illustrations by Gecko Limited and Roger Penwill
Book design by Gecko Limited
Printed and bound by Scotprint, Haddington

Acknowledgements
The Author and Publishers are grateful to the following for permission to reproduce copyright material: Faber & Faber for 'Vergissmeinnicht' by Keith Douglas and an extract from *Waiting for Godot* by Samuel Beckett; Anvil Press for 'Recognition' by Carol Ann Duffy, Random House UK Ltd/Methuen for an extract from *A Streetcar Named Desire* by Tennessee Williams; Greene & Heaton Ltd for an extract from *The Typists*, by Murray Schisgal; A M Heath/Estate of Sonia Orwell, for an extract from *The Road to Wigan Pier* by George Orwell.

Every effort has been made to contact owners of copyright material, but if any have been inadvertently overlooked, the Publishers will be pleased to make the necessary arrangements at the earliest opportunity.

Contents

How this book will help you
by Steve Jeffrey

Exam practice — how to answer questions better

This book will help you to improve your grade in your AS English Language and Literature examination.

It contains a range of typical questions covering Prose fiction and Non-fiction, Poetry, Drama, Speech and Directed writing, and provides **detailed guidance on how to structure and plan your answers** to such questions.

Reading through this book **will help you with your examination technique** and will enable you to score high marks under exam conditions.

The first six chapters focus on specific kinds of texts and are broken down into four separate elements. The final chapter contains further practice questions to help you to assess your progress.

① Typical exam questions

Each chapter contains two typical exam questions. The questions are followed by **advice** on how to tackle the questions.

The advice gives you hints on **planning your answer** and **specific terms** you can use to deal with the particular type of text.

② Extracts from students' answers at Grade C and Grade A

I have chosen an extract from a Grade C answer in response to the first exam question. I comment on the good points in the answer and then **give ideas as to how the candidate could have improved the answer** to lift it beyond a grade C. These ideas are linked to the advice given in 'How to tackle the question'.

I have chosen an extract from a Grade A answer to the second exam question. This is followed by a 'Why this scores high marks' section where **I explain why the answer achieves a Grade A**. This will enable you to demonstrate similar skills in your own answers to such questions.

③ Don't forget boxes

The Don't forget boxes highlight all the really important **skills and techniques** you need to remember when tackling a particular type of question in your exam.

④ Question to try

Each chapter closes with a further typical question for you to try. **This is a chance for you to see whether you can apply the skills and techniques highlighted in the chapter**.

Once you have written your answer, you can look at the extract from a Grade A answer provided at the back of the book and compare your answer.

I have also provided **detailed criteria as to what an examiner would look for in a Grade A and a Grade C answer** to the question. This should help you to not only assess your own answer but also find ways to improve it. You will then be able to use similar techniques in your exam which will lead to you scoring high marks for your answers.

So that you can focus on the chapters which relate directly to your exam board's specification, this chart shows you which are relevant to each specification:

How this book matches your exam board's requirements

	Chapters in 'Do Brilliantly'						
	1 Prose fiction	2 Prose non-fiction	3 Poetry	4 Drama	5 Speech and dialogue	6 Directed writing	7 Further questions
AQA SYLLABUS A							
Unit 1	✓	✓				✓	✓
Unit 2			✓				✓
Unit 3	✓				✓		✓
AQA SYLLABUS B							
Unit 1			✓				✓
Unit 2	✓				✓		✓
Unit 3	✓	✓					✓
EDEXCEL							
Unit 1	✓	✓		✓	✓		✓
Unit 2		✓				✓	✓
Unit 3	✓					✓	✓
OCR							
Unit 1	✓	✓			✓	✓	✓
Unit 2		✓				✓	✓
Unit 3	✓	✓	✓	✓	✓	✓	✓
WJEC							
Unit 1			✓				✓
Unit 2	✓	✓	✓	✓	✓	✓	✓
Unit 3	✓	✓	✓	✓	✓		✓

More Questions

The final chapter contains **more questions for you to try**.

Before you try them, re-read the relevant chapter in the book and check that you understand the **key terms** and **skills** being discussed.

Remember that the key thing is to use those approaches which are relevant to that particular type of text. Don't just apply a checklist of any terms you know.

You may wish to answer these questions under timed conditions. Begin by giving yourself 25% more time than you would have in the real examination and gradually reduce the time you allow yourself as you gain more practice.

Exam Tips

- Make sure you understand the **key words** in the exam question so that you know what it is you are being asked to do.

- Take time to **plan your work** before you start.

- **Divide the text into manageable sections** so that you can look for **similarities and differences** between them in terms of ideas, language and style.

- **Don't** simply try and identify a **checklist** of features and techniques (such as alliteration). You will not find every technique or aspect of style in each part of the text. Select those which are appropriate.

- **Look for ideas** which suggest **contrast** as a way of approaching the text and see if these contrasting ideas change as the text unfolds.

- Use **brief but relevant quotations** to support and illustrate points. Where possible try to offer further comments on the qualities suggested by the quotations.

- **Check** your answers to make sure your ideas and the way you have expressed them are clear.

- **Practise writing under timed conditions.** Begin by allowing yourself an extra 25% on the time usually given and, as you practise more answers, scale the allowed time down. Divide the time into appropriate amounts so that if, for example, you are comparing texts or if there are two parts to the question, you give yourself enough time based on the weighting of the marks. If one part of the question is worth 10 marks and the other part is worth 20 and the recommended time for both parts is one hour, you should spend 20 minutes on the 10-mark section and 40 minutes on the 20-mark section.

1 Prose fiction

You will be expected to comment on the **specific linguistic and literary** features of an extract from a set fiction text.

Typical Exam Question

The passage below is the opening to a short story, *Tickets Please*, by D H Lawrence.

There is in the Midlands a single-line tramway system which boldly leaves the country town and plunges off into the black, industrial countryside, up hill and down dale, through the long ugly villages of workmen's houses, over canals and railways, past churches perched high and noble over the smoke and shadows, through stark, grimy cold little market-places, tilting away in a rush past cinemas and shops down to the hollow where the collieries are, then up again, past a little rural church, under the ash trees, on in a rush to the terminus, the last little ugly place of industry, the cold little town that shivers on the edge of the wild, gloomy country beyond. There the green and creamy coloured tram-cars seem to pause and purr with curious satisfaction. But in a few minutes – the clock on the turret of the Co-operative Wholesale Society's shops gives the time – away it starts once more on the adventure. Again there are the reckless swoops downhill, bouncing the loops: again the chilly wait in the hill-top market-place: again the breathless slithering round the precipitous drop under the church: again the patient halts at the loops, waiting for the oncoming car: so on and on, for two long hours, till at last the city looms beyond the fat gas-works, the narrow factories draw near, we are in the sordid streets of the great town, once more we sidle to a standstill at our terminus, abashed by the great crimson and cream-coloured city cars, but still perky; jaunty somewhat dare-devil, green as a jaunty sprig of parsley out of a black colliery garden.

Discuss the use of language in this passage and its effectiveness as the opening of a short story.

In your answer you should:

- look closely at the effects created by the vocabulary;

- consider the use of the narrative voice;

- set out clearly your views on how the passage may shape our expectations of the rest of the story.

[Time allowed: 1 hour]

You should not rush into your answer but plan your work. Don't be afraid to **highlight** key words and phrases on the question paper itself.

You need to think hard about each of the prompts in the question in turn.

● Consider these points before you begin writing:

Prompt 1 'look closely at the effects created by the vocabulary'

● Can you identify certain key words or phrases which help to convey the **mood** or **tone**? Look at some of the **adjectives** that are used. Work through the passage in detail and **highlight** these. Look at the use of **colour** and the words which describe an oppressive and bleak mood (words like 'ugly', 'grimy', 'cold', 'chilly', 'sordid') compared to others such as those at the end where the colours and atmosphere seem more refreshing and exciting . Note how it is possible to find **patterns of words or phrases which echo or contrast with ideas or qualities** shown earlier in an extract.

● The passage as a whole offers a **series of contrasts** between places, moods and movement. Make sure you highlight the author's use of **opposites** like 'little' and 'fat'.

● Can you identify certain words or phrases that suggest **different types of movement** throughout the passage? Look, for example, at the start where the track 'boldly leaves' and 'plunges'; how the tram itself goes 'up' and 'under', on 'in a rush'; how it temporarily stops to 'pause' and 'purr' before there are more 'reckless swoops downhill' with 'breathless slithering'.

Prompt 2 'consider the use of the narrative voice'

● What kind of **narrative voice** can be heard? We seem to be listening to a commentary from the voice, as if we are on the journey ourselves. It is written in the **present tense** (as if it is happening at the point at which we read); it is a voice which is openly offering **judgements** on what is 'ugly' and 'gloomy' while, at the same time, trying to convey the exact **emotions** of the journey itself ('tilting away', 'in a few minutes', 'breathless', 'patient halts', 'draw near').

Prompt 3 'set out clearly your views on how the passage may shape our expectations of the rest of the story'

● What kind of **opening** is this? It offers us a panoramic view of the setting of the story and, in particular, seems to be presenting us with an overview of how industrial society has developed in the Midlands. We move from the country to the town and Lawrence describes the changes which have occurred. The tram journey itself seems to move at speed, suggesting the spread of mechanisation and industry through the region. The tram itself is a mechanised vehicle which allows the traveller to move into the industrial world (symbolised by the 'sordid streets of the great town') which seems threatening as it 'looms' with its 'fat gas-works' and factories.

● This opening could lead us to expect a story of **movement and pace**, perhaps. On the other hand, the author could use this frenetic opening as a **point of contrast** – maybe the story itself, as it unfolds, will be more focused on a particular event and character.

GOOD POINTS

> **By mentioning the idea of a camera, Peter shows he has sensed that we are being given a panoramic view of the area.**

> **Peter has realised that the passage works around the idea of contrasts. He has highlighted the contrasts in the use of colours and tried to identify a possible effect or purpose.**

> **The second paragraph has some clear, positive comments on the use of the narrative voice. It identifies that the voice offers us opinions and comments and that there is a mixture of both criticism and admiration of what is observed.**

In this passage the writer describes a tram journey from the countryside to the town. There is a lot of description about what the writer sees. There is a sense of a camera giving us a detailed look at what the writer sees. There are some contrasts between the small villages of the countryside in comparison to the 'great town' which is the destination of the journey. We move through typical features of the countryside with its villages and 'little rural church' until we see the more crowded and unpleasant large town with its 'sordid streets' and 'fat gas-works'. The author uses a range of colours to describe the different things the traveller sees; there is 'black' and 'smoke and shadows' but there is also 'crimson and cream' and 'green'. The writer seems to be describing the effects of industry on the landscape; maybe the writer is criticising the effects of pollution on the environment.

The journey seems to be a fairly quick one and we move through a number of places as we approach the city. There is a sense that we are on the journey with the writer. He uses his narrative voice to point things out to us and to offer opinions about what he sees; he tells us about 'long ugly villages' and the 'sordid streets'. He seems to dislike some of the things he sees like these and calls the gas-works 'fat' — perhaps he regards the city as spreading itself out too much. He also seems to like other things such as the 'churches perched high and noble over the smoke', perhaps suggesting a kind of fight against the industry and the town. In a way he also seems to admire the city cars and even the tram itself at the end. He describes the colours of the

cars as 'crimson' and 'cream' but also tells us that the tram when it arrives is 'still perky and jaunty, somewhat dare-devil'. While he seems to be criticising some of the things he sees, he also maybe admires some of them too.

As an opening to a short story the writing creates a rather depressing picture of the Midlands where it is set. There does not seem to be a very happy atmosphere because all the things are described in a rush and with some negative words. The writer has not introduced any main characters yet and maybe the intention is to give us a picture in our mind and to grab our attention with this unusual start.

How to score higher marks

Peter's answer shows some awareness of **contrast** between city and country but there could be more **focus** on other aspects of contrasting language. For example, Peter has noticed opposite features of buildings but has not really focused on the use of **contrasting adjectives**. Maybe he could have highlighted these words and phrases in more detail before he started writing.

Peter has suggested a possible reason for the use of colours and contrasts but leaves the idea in mid-air by suggesting it might be a piece attacking the effects of pollution. He could have explored the idea that the passage seems to be commenting on the effects of industry not just on the environment but on a way of life, a life of nature and the past. By highlighting more **key words** and **phrases** before beginning to write, Peter would have been able to develop this aspect.

In his section on the narrative voice, Peter has presented some interesting ideas but has not developed them far enough. He has not explored fully enough the **range** or **depth** of opinion that the narrative voice offers us.

Peter's final paragraph tries to deal with the requirement to assess the passage as an opening to a short story. Again, he has not **developed** his ideas far enough. He notices the depressing mood but falls back on the rather **generalised** idea that it is created to 'grab the reader's attention'. (It is important to avoid using this type of phrase in your writing because it implies you do not have any more specific ideas or comments to offer – it is something of an examination answer 'cliché'.) Peter could have explored the idea that we may be travelling from the home of a character to the city where he or she now lives. We are perhaps being introduced to the character's background and his or her move from innocence to the world of the city.

The passage below is an extract from the novel *Two on a Tower,* by Thomas Hardy. A parson is trying to coach some people from Wessex (a fictional place invented by Hardy which he imagined as a rural place with its own particular accent and dialect) to sing.

The parson announced psalm fifty-third to the tune of 'Devizes', and his voice burst forth with

> 'The Lord look'd down from Heav'n's high tower
> The sons of men to view',

in notes of rigid cheerfulness.

In this start, however, he was joined only by the girls and boys, the men furnishing but an accompaniment of ahas and hems. Mr Torkingham stopped, and Sammy Blore spoke, – 'Beg your pardon, sir, – if you'll deal mild with us a moment. What with the wind and walking, my throat's as rough as a grater; and not knowing you were going to hit up[1] that minute, I hadn't hawked,[2] and I don't think Hezzy and Nat had, either, – had ye, souls?'

'I hadn't got thorough ready, that's true,' said Hezekiah.

'Quite right of you, then, to speak,' said Mr Torkingham. 'Don't mind explaining; we are here for practice. Now clear your throats, then, and at it again.'

There was a noise as of atmospheric hoes and scrapers, and the bass contingent at last got under way with a time of its own:

'The Lard looked down vrom Heav'n's high tower!'

'Ah, that's where we are so defective – the pronunciation,' interrupted the parson. 'Now repeat after me: "The Lord look'd down from Heav'n's high tower."'

The choir repeated like an exaggerative echo: 'The Lawd look'd daown from Heav'n's high towah!'

'Better!' said the parson, in the strenuously sanguine tones of a man who got his living by discovering a bright side in things where it was not very perceptible to other people. 'But it should not be given with quite so extreme an accent; or we may be called affected by other parishes. And, Nathaniel Chapman, there's a jauntiness in your manner of singing which is not quite becoming. Why don't you sing more earnestly?'

'My conscience won't let me, sir. They say every man for himself: but, thank God, I'm not so mean as to lessen old fokes' chances by being earnest at my time o' life, and they so much nearer the need o't.'

[1] hit up: start singing.

[2] hawked: cleared throat

Comment on the use of language in the extract.

You should pay particular attention to:

• the use of dialogue in the passage;
• the use of vocabulary.

[Time allowed: 1 hour]

How to tackle this question

Before beginning to write your answer, you need to plan it. **Highlight key words or phrases.**

Prompt 1 'pay particular attention to the use of dialogue'

- Look at the use of particular **dialect words** and the way Hardy has tried to transcribe these into the written word (i.e. put spoken language as it sounds and is expressed into a written format). You should highlight these words before you begin. You could select words and phrases like 'deal mild', 'hit up', 'hawked', 'had ye', 'Lard...vrom', 'daown', 'towah', 'lessen old fokes' o't'. Such phrases show how Hardy has tried to give the members of the choir a recognisable **dialect and vocabulary**. He has tried to capture the words as they sound by misspelling them in a phonetic manner.

- He has also used **contraction** as a way of shortening words and phrases to make it seem that the speakers miss certain sounds out. He is playing on our recognition of other regional, country accents and archaic (old) pronunciation we may have heard elsewhere to help us shape a certain response to the characters. What **attitudes and values** do such features of speech convey to the reader? We may feel that the members of the choir are direct and genuine in their efforts to sing but are not as responsive to change as the parson would like. That is, the traditional dialect and accent imply that these characters are traditional and steadfast in their ways of doing things.

Prompt 2 'pay particular attention to the use of vocabulary'

- Look for use of contrast. For example, there is a clear **contrast** between the way the parson speaks and the way that the members of the choir sound. The parson is a speaker who uses **received pronunciation**. He speaks in a more formal and standard way, using the Queen's English. Contrast the way that Hardy transcribes the opening words of the song when the parson sings it with the way he does this when the choir sing the same words. The parson speaks in a gentle, polite and formal way when addressing Hezekiah: 'Quite right of you, then, to speak'. The positioning of 'then' suggests a sense of measured and calm speaking. Such examples suggest the difference in **status** between the parson and the rest of the choir. He sounds much more educated, a man of higher status. He is used to the traditional way of singing in formal settings but is far less used to the local people's way of doing things.

- What use is made of the **narrative voice** here? Hardy shapes our responses to the characters not only through the use of **dialogue** but through **authorial** comment to point up the differences between parson and choir. There is a **formality** about the vocabulary of the author's intrusion into the story. His comments tell us how **characters behave** and the **manner in which they act**. For example, the parson sings at the beginning in 'notes of rigid cheerfulness'. Perhaps Hardy is conveying the rather forced attitude the parson has to adopt to raise the effort and success of the choir. This authorial comment is echoed later on when Hardy tells us the parson was 'strenuously sanguine' and tried to discover 'a bright side in things where it was not very perceptible to other people'. Remember to try to **find patterns of words or phrases which echo or contrast** with ideas or qualities shown earlier in an extract.

Extracts from a Grade A answer

In the passage by Thomas Hardy there seems to be a clear contrast in the way the parson, Mr Torkingham, speaks compared to the other characters. First of all, he is known by a rather formal mode of address while the other members of the choir are labelled by their first or full names. This implies that he is in charge and carries some weight in the discussions. This sense of his superior status and dignity is reinforced by the way he speaks in standard English. Hardy does not spell any of his words in an unusual way, nor does he imply that he has a particular accent. Unlike the other characters his words are not affected by contractions. He is addressed as 'sir' and his authority is confirmed by the manner in which he leads the rehearsal. He gives reassurance to the choir ('Quite right of you, then, to speak') and issues gentle instructions (Now clear your throats, then, and at it again'). He uses the word 'then' twice here, implying organisation and purpose. His vocabulary seems wider, of a higher standard than that of his listeners; he uses terms such as 'so extreme an accent', 'affected' and 'jauntiness'.

Whilst the choir seem to understand his more formal terms they do not use lexis in a similar manner. They seem to have been given a fictional dialect and accent particular to the region of Wessex. Sammy Blore asks the parson to 'deal mild with us a moment'; he uses similes which appear to be understood by the rest of the choir ('my throat's as rough as a grater') and includes vocabulary outside standard English, developing his own idiolect ('hit up..hawked'). Other members of the choir also use non-standard terms; the syntax of Hezekiah's speech is not in the order we would expect and she shortens an adverb by not pronouncing the more conventionally used —ly: 'I hadn't got thorough ready, that's true'.

Hardy also uses phonetic spelling to try to illustrate the particular accent of the choir, creating a comic contrast between the way the parson sings the words of the song at the start of the passage and the performance of the other characters: 'The Lard looked down vrom Heav'ns high tower!' The idea that God resembles 'lard' adds to the humour and the exclamation mark in the quotation tries to convey how emphatic their attempt to sing is. The fact that the choir repeats the same phrase again adds to the parson's exasperation and intensifies the comic element of the passage. The parson's attempts to persuade Nathaniel Chapman to sing more earnestly are met by the character's words of wisdom — words which really have nothing to do with the parson's request. The use of archaic terms and regional dialect in his reply add to the idea that Nathaniel is an uneducated man but full of country wisdom and knowledge, a world that the parson does not really seem to know about: 'I'm not so mean as to lessen old fokes' chances by being earnest at my time o' life, and they so much nearer the need o't.'

As the author, Hardy employs vocabulary which is also very formal and standard in comparison to the choir's dialogue. His comments shape our response to the situation and produce the gentle and ironic humour which lies in the contrast between the parson and the choir. He conveys the frustrated attempts of the parson to lead the choir; Mr Torkingham sings in 'notes of rigid cheerfulness', almost forcing himself to sound positive in the light of the limited response he is getting. He tries to remain optimistic by 'discovering a bright side in things' but as the final piece of conversation shows he is not really part of the choir's world...

Why this scores high marks

- Michelle has produced a high level response. She has focused clearly on the idea of **contrast** and the ways this is achieved through the use of dialogue and choice of vocabulary. For example, she compares the dialogue between the parson and Nathaniel at the end of the extract and points up the different worlds the characters seem to inhabit. She has tried to show how the dialogue creates the gentle comic **mood** of the extract.

- She has illustrated not only what the characters say but how they say it. She has, for example, described how Mr Torkingham seems to have a particular vocabulary, how he seems to speak in a measured way in spite of his exasperation, how he addresses the choir by giving gentle instructions. She has used **brief quotations to support her comments**.

- She has tried to show how Hardy has used **phonetic spellings** and **punctuation** to convey the **dialect** and **accents** of the choir and has explored the different vocabulary used by the characters.

- She has noticed the way that the author uses vocabulary and comment to highlight the comic mood of the passage. She has noticed some **words** and **phrases** which **echo others used elsewhere** in the passage when she focuses on the attempts of the parson to put on an image of positive cheerfulness.

- Michelle makes **brief comparisons** as she goes along by inserting **phrases** such as 'unlike the other characters'. This allows her to make **short, incisive points by grouping some comparative ideas together**.

Don't forget ...

Before you begin, **plan your answer**. Always use the **prompts** to help you with your planning and with the overall structure of your answer. That is what they are there for! Highlight key words and phrases that you will want to incorporate into your answer.

Look for **contrasts** in how things are described or between characters. Compare the **status** of different characters. Try to see if they come from different worlds.

If there is **dialogue**, look hard at what characters say and how they say it.

Make **comparative points** as you go along, supported by the use of brief quotations.

Look for **echoes** and **contrasts** of certain words and phrases.

Look at the use of the **narrative voice** or the **role of the author**. Consider how these shape the reader's response to the setting or characters.

Try to explore the **mood** created by the author's choice and use of language.

If asked to comment on the **effectiveness of the opening** of a story, you need to explore what **expectations** the author may be trying to create in the mind of the reader.

When you make a point, make sure that you develop it fully enough. Don't just make a statement – **back it up with quotes from the extract** so that the examiner gets a clear understanding of the idea you are trying to get across.

Don't just say **what** the writer does – the examiner will be looking for you to explain **why** he or she does it: the **effect** he/she is trying to produce.

The passage below comes from *Jane Eyre*, by Charlotte Bronte. In it, Mr Rochester expresses his affection for his employee.

'You are a beauty, in my eyes; and a beauty just after the desire of my heart, – delicate and aerial.'

'Puny and insignificant, you mean. You are dreaming, sir – or you are sneering. For God's sake, don't be ironical!'

'I will make the world acknowledge you a beauty, too,' he went on, while I really became uneasy at the strain he had adopted; because I felt he was either deluding himself, or trying to delude me. 'I will attire my Jane in satin and lace, and she shall have roses in her hair; and I will cover the head I love best with a priceless veil.'

'And then you won't know me, sir; and I shall not be your Jane Eyre any longer, but an ape in a harlequin's jacket, – a jay in borrowed plumes. I would as soon see you, Mr Rochester, tricked out in stage-trappings, as myself clad in a court-lady's robe; and I don't call you handsome, sir, though I love you most dearly: far too dearly to flatter you. Don't flatter me.'

He pursued his theme, however, without noticing my deprecation. 'This very day I shall take you in the carriage to Millcote, and you must choose some dresses for yourself. I told you we shall be married in four weeks. The wedding is to take place quietly, in the church down below yonder; and then I shall waft you away at once to town. After a brief stay there, I shall bear my treasure to regions nearer the sun: to French vineyards and Italian plains; and she shall see whatever is famous in old story and in modern record: she shall taste, too, of the life of cities; and she shall learn to value herself by just comparison with others.'

'Shall I travel? – and with you, sir?'

'You shall sojourn at Paris, Rome, and Naples: at Florence, Venice and Vienna: all the ground I have wandered over shall be re-trodden by you: wherever I stamped my hoof, your sylph's foot shall step also. Ten years since, I flew through Europe half mad; with disgust, hate, and rage, as my companions: now I will revisit it healed and cleansed, with a very angel as my comforter.'

I laughed at him as he said this, 'I am not an angel,' I asserted; 'and I will not be one till I die: I will be myself.'

Consider the use of language in the passage.

You should pay particular attention to:
• the use of dialogue;
• the use of vocabulary.

[Time allowed: 1 hour]

After writing your answer, turn to page 85 for help with marking it.

2 Prose non-fiction

You will be expected to study extracts from non-fiction and to comment on them in terms of their **linguistic** and **literary** features.

You will be asked to **analyse and comment on different types** of non-fiction texts. These could include advertisements, diaries, travel writing, reviews, newspaper or magazine features, or biography.

You may also be asked to **compare** the linguistic and literary features of such non-fiction pieces to prose texts or transcripts of spontaneous or written speech (see Chapter 7, page 67).

Typical Exam Question

The two extracts below contain text from two advertisements that appeared in a broadsheet newspaper.

Advertisement A

TCP HOLDINGS PLC is a major financial group based in Cardiff with offices throughout the UK including London.

As part of our ongoing expansion we now require an experienced and pro-active Marketing and Development Director within our general commercial insurance, life and pensions brokerage. This post has dual responsibilities in both Cardiff and London. In this key role you will control all marketing and development activity for the company, building positive relationships with established and prospective clients throughout the corporate sector. You will identify new opportunities and also be the 'door opener' for our organisation, bringing your considerable financial, interpersonal and management skills to bear in the preparation and presentation of tenders for new business from companies with a turnover in excess of £1 million. In meeting your objectives you will be required to promote both yourself and TCP Holdings in a professional and effective way throughout the Welsh business community, working closely with the intermediary sector, including venture capitalists, banks, economic development departments of local authorities and the WDA. The building of a meaningful prospect database, the organisation of a corporate hospitality programme and the consistent development of the company's profile are all integral parts of this new and exciting role within our company.

This is a challenge that rarely comes along...

If you have drive, excellent all-round marketing skills and truly relish the challenges of winning new business then we would very much like to hear from you.

Please send a full CV, stating your current salary and benefits, to the Personnel Director, TCP Holdings plc, 1 Green Street, London, E1 2AB

Advertisement B

┌─SHAPING
│ COMMUNICATIONS
│ STRATEGY┐
└──────────┘

Internal Communications Manager

London/Kent Borders
c.£40,000 plus benefits

At **Savers** our success has been built on a progressive corporate strategy and committed people. Our plans to convert to plc this year mean we've a great deal to look forward to – and even more to offer. Critical to our success is the development of our Internal Communications function, which is why we now need an experienced and capable individual to take on the challenge.

This is a high profile and demanding role – with the opportunity to make distinctive cultural changes within the organisation. You'll take a hands-on approach – planning and implementing an effective internal communications strategy which supports our expanding business programme as well as managing a team.

With the ability to think on your feet, you'll develop a thorough understanding of the communication needs of the Savers group, and form part of a wider corporate communications team. Above all, offering innovative solutions appropriate to a diverse audience will be your biggest challenge.

A leading light in your present company, you're looking for the chance to grow with a truly progressive company. You already have at least 3 years' middle management experience in a customer facing business with high standards of internal communication. Practical knowledge of all media and the operations of a plc in the retail/financial services sector as essential. You have first rate interpersonal/ communication skills and an excellent track record in team management. You will ideally be a graduate in a communications discipline, or of graduate calibre.

It's a challenging role and offers unrivalled scope for career development. Benefits are generous and all you would expect from a leading financial services organisation. To apply, please write with CV, and details of your current package to Jackie Smith, HR Service Manager, Savers Building Society, Corporate HQ, Exchange Street, London W2 OTT.

Closing date for receipt of applications is 23 June 2006.

Savers is an equal opportunities employer. We welcome applications from people with disabilities, from all races, religions and from both sexes.

Comment on the style of both advertisements. In your answer you should:
• consider the use of language;
• consider the techniques they use to try and persuade the reader to apply.

[Time allowed: 1 hour]

You should not rush into your answer but plan your work. Don't be afraid to **highlight** key words and phrases on the question paper itself.

Divide each text into **smaller sections** so that you can look for **similarities** and **differences** between them.

Before you begin consider these other points:

- **Who** is each advertisement intended for and what is its **context** and **purpose**?

- What kind of **language** is used to portray the company's **image**? What kind of **register** is used? Is the text trying to use humour, friendliness or jargon, for example?

- What kind of **mode of address** is used? Does it change as the text progresses?

- What kind of **language** is used to make the post sound appealing? Does it use a particular **semantic field** (particular patterns of words which can be grouped together)? Remember that just as there can be patterns of imagery in literary texts (see other chapters), it is also possible to see specific types of words appearing in certain types of non-literary texts.

- Are there any particular **techniques** that the advertisement seems to use to persuade the reader? For example, some advertisements offer '**aspirational**' ideas, encouraging the reader to believe they can **achieve particular goals or a certain lifestyle**.

Look at other aspects of language. Sometimes advertisements will use **repetition** or **signpost specific words** (think of the number of times you come across the word 'new' in advertisements).

Look for specific use of **abstract nouns**, words which are used to name things we can not see or touch. They can convey a sense of the aspirational.

Consider if any particular **adjectives** (describing words) are used to portray a particular **idea** or **image**.

See if any '**buzz**' **words** are used, that is words which seem to be in fashion at a particular time.

- Does the advert seem to offer a particular **vision**? Sometimes advertisements will trade on nostalgia by painting a picture of the past: others look to the future in a positive and uplifting way.

- **Don't waste space and time** by commenting on **graphology** (design) or the use of fonts. **Your focus should be on the language of the text**.

Extracts from a Grade C answer

GOOD POINTS

Tom has tried to offer some awareness of the audience but has not defined its type fully.

He has spotted some aspects of the mode of address.

Both advertisements are aimed at posh people because they are the sort of people who read broadsheet papers. Both advertisements are upmarket and speak to the readers in a very direct way. The first piece of text makes the post sound exciting by using words like 'pro-active' and 'key role' while the second piece of text uses phrases like 'challenge' and 'high profile and demanding role'. Passage A tries to persuade the reader that it too is offering an 'exciting role' and says that the person who gets the job will be carrying out an important responsibility. Passage B also describes that the successful candidate will be an important person already 'a leading light'.

Both advertisements try to make their companies sound dynamic and prepared for a busy and positive future. TCP Holdings talk about their 'ongoing expansion' where the postholder must 'relish' challenges. Savers discusses its 'progressive corporate strategy' and tries to make candidates interested by outlining how they have 'a great deal to look forward to'.

The first advertisement uses a hook or catchline at the end to try and remind the reader of the opportunity they have got: 'This is a challenge that rarely comes along' suggests you may never get this kind of chance again. The second advertisement does not use a logo like this but at the end of the text tries to show it is a caring company by saying how it welcomes 'applications from people with disabilities, from all races, religions and from both sexes'. This may make some kinds of reader feel more attracted to Savers...

> **Tom has used brief quotation to explain how both companies express the nature of the job and to try and show how both advertisements convey an image of the company and the vision they have for the future.**

> **He has tried to compare the language of both advertisements to show how each seeks to engage with and to appeal to different kinds of reader.**

How to score higher marks

Tom has made some competent if rather obvious points. His ideas are good but lack precision. For example, he defines the **audience** in a rather generalised way; he should think more about the age range of his readers, their social status, lifestyle, work background and gender. Similarly, he has not fully explored the **purpose** and **context** of the advertisements, that is the attempt to suggest that these are high-powered jobs requiring experienced and strongly motivated employees.

Tom has not really probed the **mode of address** as much as he could; for example, the way the second person ('you') is used in both advertisements and the way the reader is 'told' what they will be like to make everything seem active ('you will control all marketing' or 'you'll develop a thorough understanding') by the use of the future tense.

Tom could explore the use of **semantic fields** and **'buzz' words** a lot more. Both advertisements are noticeable for their use of business or corporate **jargon** in order to try and persuade the audience that they are impressive companies in their respective markets. Such jargon creates some complex and compound vocabulary such as 'middle management experience in a customer facing business with high standards of internal communication' or 'bringing your considerable financial, interpersonal and management skills to bear in the preparation and presentation of tenders for new business'.

 Tom could also explore the use of **abstract nouns** and **adjectives** more in both pieces of text. For example, the first advertisement employs **nouns** like 'responsibilities', 'opportunities', 'building', 'organisation' and 'profile'; the second one uses terms like 'strategy', 'success', 'opportunity' and 'standards'. Both advertisements use identical terms like 'challenge'. This **pattern of words** tries to suggest that the world of finance and business has its own vocabulary and to participate in it you need to share the same vocabulary and outlook as the language used here. The terms suggest something to aim for, something that can only be measured by company and individuals in a shared way. **Adjectives** are also used too to add excitement to the prospective posts; Passage A employs words like 'pro-active' and 'new' while Passage B uses words like 'progressive' and 'unrivalled' to stress the **vision** and **image** of the company.

Typical Exam Question

The passage below is taken from *The Road to Wigan Pier* written by George Orwell, published in 1937. In it he describes his impressions of a group of coalminers.

It is impossible to watch the 'fillers' at work without feeling a pang of envy for their toughness. It is a dreadful job that they do, an almost superhuman job by the standards of an ordinary person. For they are not only shifting monstrous quantities of coal, they are also doing it in a position that doubles or trebles the work. They have got to remain kneeling all the while – they could hardly rise from their knees without hitting the ceiling – and you can easily see by trying it what a tremendous effort this means. Shovelling is comparatively easy when you are standing up, because you can use your knee and thigh to drive the shovel along; kneeling down, the whole of the strain is thrown upon your arm and belly muscles. And the other conditions do not exactly make things easier. There is the heat – it varies, but in some mines it is suffocating – and the coal dust that stuffs up your throat and nostrils and collects along your eyelids, and the unending rattle of the conveyor belt, which in that confined space is rather like the rattle of a machine gun. But the fillers look and work as though they were made of iron. They really do look like iron-hammered iron statues – under the smooth coat of coal dust which clings to them from head to foot. It is only when you see miners down the mine and naked that you realise what splendid men they are. Most of them are small (big men are at a disadvantage in that job) but nearly all of them have the most noble bodies; wide shoulders tapering to slender supple waists, and small pronounced buttocks and sinewy thighs, with not an ounce of waste flesh anywhere. In the hotter mines they wear only a pair of thin drawers, clogs and knee-pads; in the hottest mines of all, only the clogs and knee-pads. You can hardly tell by the look of them whether they are young or old.

They may be any age up to sixty or even sixty-five, but when they are black and naked they all look alike. No one could do their work who had not a young man's body, and a figure fit for a guardsman at that; just a few pounds of extra flesh on the waist-line, and the constant bending would be impossible. You can never forget that spectacle once you have seen it – the line of bowed, kneeling figures, sooty black all over, driving their huge shovels under the coal with stupendous force and speed.

Write a critical appreciation of this passage. In your answer you should:
• comment on the mood;
• comment on linguistic and literary features.

[Time allowed: 1 hour]

How to tackle this question

Remember to plan and **highlight key words or phrases**.

Remember to divide the passage into **sections** so that you can look for **similarities** and **differences** between them.

Before you begin you should also :
• Consider the **mood** and **mode of address** in the passage.
• Explore the **descriptive use of language** and the **qualities** it creates. For example, there is a strong degree of physicality suggested by some of the words and phrases.

See if there are any **patterns of imagery** in the extract. Try to assess what **impressions** they create. Do they contribute to the **mood** in any particular way?

Look at other **uses of language** such as **phrasing** and **syntax** (the way sentences are constructed).

Extracts from a Grade A answer

Orwell writes in a tone of admiration for the miners, an admiration which not only takes in the arduous nature of their job but also their physical appearance and staying power; it is almost a sense of pride in masculinity that runs through the extract. He seems to place the miners on a pedestal, calling them 'superhuman' and, later, 'noble'; they may work below the earth but their spirit rises far above it. In a sense there is a note of frustration, a sense of realising his difference to them: 'without feeling a pang of envy for their toughness'. Orwell addresses the reader in a personal way (by using 'you') almost as if he is taking us round a picture or tableau in a documentary style. His commentary is not afraid to be judgemental: 'It is a dreadful job they do'. He clearly wishes us to share his view of the miners by reassuring us that they are 'splendid men'. He exudes a strong degree of sympathy which he tries to make us share and appreciate: 'They have got to remain kneeling all the time...and you can easily see by trying it what a tremendous effort this means.'

Orwell employs descriptive language to try and show the physical elements of the environment they work in; he mentions the 'heat' and the 'coal dust' and again tries to make us share it by describing the bodily impact of these elements: 'in some mines it is suffocating' and dust 'stuffs up your throat'. The unpleasant echoes of 'suffocating' and 'stuffs' express the conditions the miners work in. The descriptive language is also used to describe the physical appearance of the miners. There seems to be an almost voyeuristic appreciation of their bodies, a latent sexual interest: 'wide shoulders tapering to slender supple waists'. He seems to admire their godlike power and energy as they use their 'huge shovels' with 'stupendous force and speed'. The miners have been given an almost classical heroic stature in spite of their appearance. While they may be hidden by coal dust they also represent some form of primitive and superhuman force. There is something noble and permanent about them. Orwell uses metallic images to suggest their inner strength and almost mechanical precision: 'They really do look like iron-hammered iron statues'. This type of comparison reinforces the sense of awe that the writer exhibits.

Orwell expresses himself in a direct and direct manner. There is little use of qualifying statements or phrasing. He makes strong assertions like 'It is impossible', 'It is a dreadful job', 'They really do look like' and 'Most of them are'; there is sense of certainty and conviction, as if he is trying to persuade the reader to accept that this is the real world and we should appreciate and admire the hardship and dignity of working people...

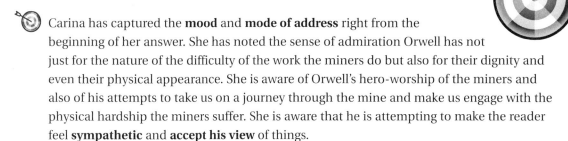

Why this scores high marks

Carina has captured the **mood** and **mode of address** right from the beginning of her answer. She has noted the sense of admiration Orwell has not just for the nature of the difficulty of the work the miners do but also for their dignity and even their physical appearance. She is aware of Orwell's hero-worship of the miners and also of his attempts to take us on a journey through the mine and make us engage with the physical hardship the miners suffer. She is aware that he is attempting to make the reader feel **sympathetic** and **accept his view** of things.

Carina has explored the **use of descriptive language** well and used **brief quotations** effectively. She has conveyed the physicality not just of the environment but also the men's physical appearance and made some interesting comments on the possible **effects** such **description** has by using the ideas of voyeurism and masculinity.

She has also tried to comment on the **use of particular images** such as the references to 'superhuman' and 'iron'. She suggests some of the possible **qualities** that these comparisons imply. She notes the idea of godlike status given to the miners and makes a perceptive comment of her own that while the miners may work below the ground they are give the stature of heavenly powers.

Carina has also tried to deal with **other aspects of language** such as the style of **phrasing** and **expression** although perhaps in a rather imprecise style. She does note the confident and positive **tone** that Orwell employs and groups several examples of these together. She tries to offer some **reasons** for this style such as the possibility that Orwell is trying to persuade us through a sense of self-conviction and force.

Don't forget ...

Always divide the passage into **sections** so you can see **similarities** and **differences** between them and remember to **highlight key words and phrases**.

Work out the **audience**, **context** and **purpose** of the piece of writing.

Comment on **semantic fields** (patterns of words), **patterns of imagery** and **descriptive language**.

Try to comment on **other uses of language** such as **phrasing, syntax, abstract nouns** and **adjectives**.

Consider the **techniques** the writer uses to try and **persuade** the reader about **ideas** and **attitudes**.

The extracts below are taken from the diaries of two explorers of Antarctica. The first passage is the final entry of Captain Scott's diary written in 1912. The second passage is taken from the diary of Richard E Byrd written in the 1930s. Scott did not survive: Byrd did.

Passage A

Monday, March 19. Lunch. We camped with difficulty last night, and were dreadfully cold till after our supper of cold penirnican and biscuit and a half a pannikin of cocoa cooked over the spirit. Then, contrary to expectation, we got warm and slept well. To-day we started in the usual dragging manner. Sledge dreadfully heavy. We are 15 miles from the depot and ought to get there in three days. What progress!

We have two days' food but barely a day's fuel. All our feet are getting bad - Wilson's best, my right foot worst, left all right. There is no chance to nurse one's feet till we can get hot food into us. Amputation is the least I can hope for now, but will the trouble spread? That is the serious question. The weather doesn't give us a chance - the wind from N to NW and –40 temp. today.

Wednesday, March 21. Got within 11 miles of depot Monday night; had to lay up all yesterday in severe blizzard. To-day forlorn hope, Wilson and Bowers going to depot for fuel.

Thursday, March 22 and 23. Blizzard bad as ever – Wilson and Bowers unable to start – tomorrow last chance – no fuel and only one or two of food left – must be near the end. Have decided it shall be natural – we shall march for the depot with or without our effects and die in our tracks.

Thursday, March 29. Since the 21st we have had a continuous gale from WSW and SW. We had fuel to make two cups of tea apiece and bare food for two days on the 20th. Every day we have been ready to start for our depot 11 miles away, but outside the door of the tent it remains a scene of whirling drift. I do not think we can hope for any better things now. We shall stick it out to the end, but we are getting weaker, of course, and the end cannot be far.

It seems a pity, but I do not think I can write more.   R.SCOTT.

Last entry.

For God's sake look after our people.

Passage B

JUNE 1ST WAS A FRIDAY. A black Friday for me. The nightmare left me, and about 9 o'clock in the morning I awakened with a violent start, as if I had been thrown down a well in my sleep. I found myself staring wildly into the darkness of the shack, not knowing where I was. The weakness that filled my body when I turned in the sleeping bag and tried to throw the flashlight on my wrist watch was an eloquent reminder. I was Richard E. Byrd, United States Navy (Ret.), temporarily sojourning at Latitude 80° 08' South, and not worth a damn to myself or anybody else. My mouth was dry and tasted foul. God, I was thirsty. But I had hardly strength to move. I clung to the sleeping bag, which was the only source of comfort and warmth left to me, and mournfully debated the little that might be done.

But you must have faith – you must have faith in the outcome, I whispered to myself. It is like a flight, a flight into another unknown. You start and you cannot turn back. You must go on and on and on, trusting your instruments, the course you have plotted on the charts, and the reasonableness of events. Whatever goes wrong will be mostly of your own making; if it is to be tragedy, then it will be the common-place tragedy of human vulnerability.

I WON'T EVEN ATTEMPT to recall all the melancholy thoughts that drifted through my mind that long afternoon. But I can say truthfully that at no time did I have any feeling of resignation. My whole being rebelled against my low estate. As the afternoon wore on, I felt myself sinking. Now I became alarmed. This was not the first time I had ever faced death. It had confronted me many times in the air. But then it had seemed altogether different. In flying things happen fast: you make a decision; the verdict crowds you instantly; and, when the invisible and neglected passenger comes lunging into the cockpit, he is but one of countless distractions. But now death was a stranger sitting in a darkened room, secure in the knowledge that he would be there when I was gone.

Great waves of fear, a fear I had never known before, swept through me and settled deep within. But it wasn't the fear of suffering or even of death itself. It was a terrible anxiety over the consequences to those at home if I failed to return. I had done a damnable thing in going to Advance Base, I told myself. Also, during those hours of bitterness, I saw my whole life pass in review. I realized how wrong my sense of values had been and how I had failed to see that the simple, homely, unpretentious things of life are the most important.

Compare the style of these two extracts. In your answer you should:
• consider the tone in both passages;
• comment on the use of language in both passages.

[Time allowed: 1 hour]

After writing your answer, turn to page 86 for help with marking it.

You will be expected to analyse and comment on different types of poems from different periods.

To do well, you need to be able to comment on the **linguistic** features of poems: for example, a question may involve discussing **register** (the type of language used) and **syntax** (the order in which ideas are expressed) as well as **imagery** and the use of **rhythm** and **sounds**.

Typical Exam Question

The extract below appears in *The Nun's Priest's Tale*, by Geoffrey Chaucer. In it, Chauntecleer, a cockerel, tells his partner, Pertelote, that he is not afraid of dreams and has better things to do with his time.

'Now let us speke of myrthe, and stynte al this.
Madame Pertelote, so have I blis,
Of o thyng God hath sent me large grace;
For whan I se the beautee of youre face,
Ye been so scarlet reed aboute youre yen,
It maketh al my drede for to dyen;
For al so siker as *In principio,*
Muller est hominis Confusio,
Madame, the sentence of this Latyn is,
"Womman is mannes joye and al his blis."
For whan I feele a-nyght your softe syde,
Al be it that I may nat on yow ryde,
For that oure perche is maad so narwe, allas!
I am so ful of joye and of solas,
That I diffye both sweven and dreem.'
And with that word he fley doun fro the beem,
For it was day, and eke his hennes alle,
And with a chuk he gan hem for to calle,
For he hadde founde a corn, lay in the yerd.
Real he was, he was namoore aferd.
He fethered Pertelote twenty tyme,
And trad hire eke as ofte, er it was pryme.
He looketh as it were a grym leoun,
And on his toos he rometh up and doun;
Hym deigned nat to sette his foot to grounde.
He chukketh whan he hath a corn yfounde,
And to hym rennen thanne his wyves alle.
Thus roial, as a prince is in his halle,
Leve I this Chauntecleer in his pasture,
And after wol I telle his aventure.

Consider the style of this extract. In your answer you should comment on:
• the presentation of Chauntecleer;
• description and tone.

[Time allowed: 1 hour]

How to tackle this question

You should remember to divide the extract into shorter, more manageable sections (say 6 to 8 lines each) so that you can look for **similarities** and **differences** between them. This will allow you to comment on the **structure** and **progression** of the passage.

Don't be afraid to **highlight key words and phrases** on the question paper itself.

Consider some of these further points <u>before</u> you begin writing:

- Think about the **nature of the voice**. In other words, who is speaking to us? It may be the author, a character or a narrator. The use of the word 'I' does not always mean that it is the poet expressing the ideas. The narrator may be a character we **cannot trust** or who is blind to his or her faults.

- This sense that the narrator cannot see his or her faults but we can may create **irony**, a process by which the audience or other characters are aware of something that the narrator is not.

- Think about the **context** of the poem: the situation or narrative situation in which it is set. This may also create **irony** or it may sometimes mean, as it can do in prose and drama, that a character uses language which is inappropriate for the context, highlighting his or her lack or awareness or creating humour.

- Look at the **register**, the type of language that is used and the **tone** or **mood** that created it. Try to see if the mood or tone changes as you look at different sections.

- Look at the use of **syntax** and the **mode of address**. Are words expressed in a formal way? Is the character speaking in an **appropriate way** to us or another character bearing in mind the **context** or situation?

- Try to comment on the **ideas**, **mood** or **qualities** suggested by the **imagery** (the metaphors or similes used). Sometimes the qualities suggested by imagery can also be **ironic**, casting a humorous light on a narrator or character.

GOOD POINTS

Craig has tried to address some aspects of the question in a direct and ordered way by using paragraphs. He makes appropriate and competent comments about Chauntecleer's mood and apparent self-satisfaction.

He identifies Chauntecleer's rather arrogant attitude in the way he tries to show his knowledge and education. He also senses that this is a way for Chauntecleer to exert mental as well as physical control in the extract, perhaps not quite developing this point when 'superiority' is mentioned.

Craig also notices differences between sections and makes the point that Chauntecleer is not quite as clever as he thinks he is when he ignores the potential warnings signified by dreams.

Craig spots some aspects of mood and tone and grasps the humour of the passage.

In this passage we see that Chauntecleer seems to be rather happy and contented. He speaks in a rather formal way to Pertelote ('Now let vs speke of myrthe... Madame Pertelote'); he tries to compliment her on her beauty and it is ironic to see the way that the two birds are turned into rather formal lovers. Chaucer has used personification to do this. Chauntecleer tries to show off — again in a humorous way — when he attempts to show his knowledge and education. He quotes Latin in order to show his sense of superiority. However, as the passage progresses, we see that he is not as educated as he thinks. He forgets about the possible warnings created by dreams as his sexual desires get the better of him. He says that he defies 'sweven and dreem'.

There is some humour created by the descriptive parts of the passage. For example, when Chauntecleer compliments Pertelote on the 'scarlet reed about youre yen' it would seem less attractive to us if we praised a human for the red colour around their eyes. His mood becomes very proud when he walks around the yard; he seems to be like a king — 'Real he was'. He seems to have become confident and proud, scared of nothing. We can sense this when he is compared to a 'grym leoun'. He seems like he is king of the animals in his own little world, in control of his life and situation. All his hens run towards him and he feels in control of them too.

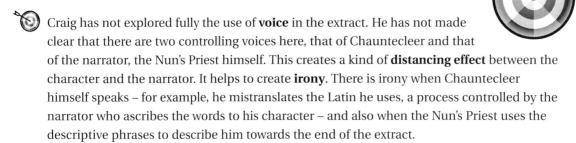

Craig has not explored fully the use of **voice** in the extract. He has not made clear that there are two controlling voices here, that of Chauntecleer and that of the narrator, the Nun's Priest himself. This creates a kind of **distancing effect** between the character and the narrator. It helps to create **irony**. There is irony when Chauntecleer himself speaks – for example, he mistranslates the Latin he uses, a process controlled by the narrator who ascribes the words to his character – and also when the Nun's Priest uses the descriptive phrases to describe him towards the end of the extract.

Craig has also not fully developed the **use of irony** created by the **context** or narrative situation. He has touched on matters briefly, like the use of **personification**, but has not really probed the idea of **parody** (to mock something by mimicking its features and convention) of the courtly love tradition or the absurdity of two creatures addressing each other in human terms. This is an area that Craig could develop.

Craig has shown some awareness of the use of **register** and **syntax** and notes the rather formal way that Chauntecleer addresses Pertelote. He could have developed this sense of formality, as if Chauntecleer regards himself as some kind of teacher educating his rather less informed partner. For example, he could have commented on the first line itself which has a very emphatic and even monosyllabic style, as if Chauntecleer is trying to reinforce his authority in every word. He could have probed the **differences** in the use of **register** in later sections where Chauntecleer's language becomes gentler and tries to be absurdly romantic: he mentions her 'scarlet yen' and her 'softe syde' but seems unable to sustain this generous language as his **tone** switches back to himself and his rather self-centred concerns: 'It maketh al my drede for to dyen…I am so ful of joye and solas'.

Craig could have explored the use of **imagery** in a little more depth. If he had recognised that the **voice** switches back to the Nun's Priest himself he could have detected the rather **ironic** qualities suggested by the comparisons. The narrator is exaggerating Chauntecleer's degree of self-importance by comparing a mere bird to the king of the wild animals. The narrator's **tone** is reinforced by his use of the words 'Hym deigned nat to sette his foote to the grounde'. To consolidate this impression the narrator also compares the character to a prince, another royal figure. While this reinforces the idea that Chauntecleer is a **parody** of some vain human creature, it also conveys the sense of authority and power he thinks he has; he is blind to his own limitations, an idea clearly shown earlier in his misunderstanding of the Latin he quoted.

The poem below is called *A View from Westminster Bridge: London 1802* and was written by William Wordsworth.

Earth has not anything to show more fair:
Dull would he be of soul who could pass by
A sight so touching in its majesty:
This City now doth like a garment wear
The beauty of the morning; silent, bare;
Ships, towers, domes, theatres, and temples lie
Open unto the fields and to the sky;
All bright and glittering in the smokeless air.
Never did sun more beautifully steep
In his first splendour, valley, rock, or hill;
Ne'er saw I, never felt, a calm so deep!
The river glideth at his own sweet will:
Dear God! the very houses seem asleep;
And all that mighty heart is lying still!

Write a critical appreciation of the poem. In your answer you should:
• consider the use of imagery;
• comment on features of language and form.

[Time allowed: 1 hour]

How to tackle this question

- Remember, even with a piece which seems as short as this, to divide the poem into **sections** so you can compare **similarities** and **differences** between them.

- Look at the **use of voice** in the poem. Is the voice a character, an unreliable narrator, or does it seem to be the personal voice of the poet?

- When considering the **use of language**, see if there are any **patterns of imagery**. Remember that imagery is an all-embracing term. It includes descriptive language (such as the use of adjectives like 'silent' and 'bare'), **metaphors** (a direct comparison which is not literally true such as the idea in the poem that London has 'a mighty heart' which 'is lying still') and **similes** (a comparison which uses 'like' or 'as': for example, 'This City now doth like a garment wear/The beauty of the morning'). Imagery can also include **personification** where an object is given human qualities. Here, for example, the City is seen as an active and living figure.

- It is sometimes worth exploring **symbols** or **motifs** in your answer. This is when a particular object or feature represents a certain idea or quality as a kind of sustained metaphor. In the Wordsworth poem, for example, the image of light could be associated with something pure and timeless.

- Look out for particular **recognisable poetic forms**. For example, the poem concerned here is a **sonnet**. This should trigger certain ideas suggested through the study of other sonnets. The form requires the writer to express ideas and thoughts in a tightly defined space. There tends to be a set pattern of structure: the first eight lines (the octet or octave), followed by a turn or volta (that is a change in mood, direction of thought or argument), ending in a sestet (the final six lines). It is also important when dividing the poem into short sections not to deal solely with the octet and sestet.

The octet itself is made up of two quatrains (four rhyming lines).

- Be aware of the **rhyme scheme** – but avoid wasting time on pointless identification of it. See if it contributes anything to the meaning.

- Be aware that poems are meant to be **read aloud** and that writers may try to achieve certain effects through the **use of sounds, different uses of register** and **syntax**.

Extracts from a Grade A answer

This sonnet begins in a direct and confident manner with the assertive voice of the poet making a sweeping and enthusiastic statement: 'Earth has not anything to show more fair'. He is sure of his ground and can declare his views with a sense of authority, as if he is in a privileged position of knowledge. He knows not only about the sight before him but about human nature and sensibilities: 'Dull would he be of soul who could pass by...' Immediately there is a juxtaposition of images suggesting light and darkness ('fair' and 'dull'), of ideas suggesting the outer material world (the view) and the inner world of individuals ('soul'). There is a sense that the view itself will bring the soul to life, that inner and outer worlds should meet in appreciation of the beauty.

The City is personified and given the air of royalty and poise ('its majesty'); the figure seems to be dressed in a spiritual beauty, wearing a 'garment'; at the same time it is 'silent' and 'bare', as if the garment is ethereal showing an inner world again. Wordsworth uses a cumulative effect ('Ships, towers, domes, theatres and temples') as if contemplating the features of the personified City, appreciating its details and poise. The earlier pattern of images suggesting light are reinforced by the descriptive terms 'bright and glittering' at the close of the octave. Other words convey images of freedom and purity, an untouched beauty before the city comes to normal life ('open' and 'smokeless'). It almost seems that the City is at one with Nature, meeting the elements of 'sky' and 'fields' in a panoramic unity. Indeed, it is given qualities of something untainted and pure, as if uncontaminated by life and experience yet.

The sestet seems to develop this idea further and suggest that it is almost an Eden. The emphatic use of 'Never' conveys this view and echoes the assertive opening line that the Earth has never looked fairer — except that we have moved from the present tense of the first line to the past tense in line nine: 'Never did sun more beautifully steep....' The use of the symbolic sun, a motif suggesting light again, suggests giving life to some pure form. It not only gives life to the world of Nature ('valley, rock, or hill') but to the world of the City too: town and country are united. The poet reinforces the use of Never on line nine with its repeated if contracted form two lines later; the parallel use of the construction also switches the focus of the poem away from the hitherto unseen view of the city to the hitherto unfelt celebration of the poet's soul; he feels a kind of inner contemplation, 'calm', and satisfaction he has not experienced before. The sounds are gentle ('The river glideth at his own sweet will') but suddenly the final two lines burst out into a kind of celebratory passion, a kind of disbelief that there is life about to burst forth; we close with the personified figure of the City, a wonder at 'that mighty heart is lying still'.

Why this scores high marks

- Carly has produced a promising high level response. She has managed to convey a sense of the **progression** of the passage as well as the sense of mood and meaning.

- Carly has quickly addressed the ideas of **form** by mentioning that the poem is a sonnet and shown awareness of the octave and sestet format.

- She is aware that the writer is speaking directly to us in a personal **voice**. There is no sense of a narrator or unreliable character here.

- She has considered the **mode of address** and the **tone** behind his words right from the beginning of the piece. She is aware that the writer seems to be confident and assertive. She is also careful to pick up the idea of the **tone** in the sestet as well as the octet in the way that she compares lines 1 and 9. She has commented on **similarities** and **differences** between **sections**.

- Carly has clearly identified and commented on particular **techniques** such as **personification** and tried to explore its effects on meaning and interpretation.

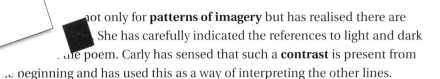

core higher marks

not only for **patterns of imagery** but has realised there are
She has carefully indicated the references to light and dark
the poem. Carly has sensed that such a **contrast** is present from
the beginning and has used this as a way of interpreting the other lines.

Without being excessive, Carly has explored the idea of a possible **motif** in discussing the use of the 'sun'. It implies to her that the poet sees this situation as not just another day but as something symbolic and deeper.

Because Carly has worked on the idea of **contrast** she has not only spotted these in terms of the **imagery** but in terms of **ideas**. She mentions areas such as inner and outer worlds, present and past, town and country. Exploring contrasts can open up **meanings**.

Carly has also tried to include some references to **other uses of language** such as parallel constructions, sounds, cumulative effects, and has tried to link their presence to aspects of **mood** and **meaning**. She has not just provided a checklist.

Don't forget ...

Remember to divide the poem into sections so you can look for **similarities** and **differences** between them.

Look out for particular recognisable poetic forms such as the sonnet.

Try to work out the **voice** of the poem. Is it the personal voice of the poet? Is it a character or an unreliable narrator?

Look at the use of **register**, the mode of address and syntax.

Look for the use of **contrast**, especially in terms of ideas or language.

Look for the use of **irony** and the **effects** it creates. Does it create humour? Does it affect our interpretation of a particular character or idea?

Look for patterns of **imagery** or **contrasting** images. What kinds of meaning do they create? Remember that imagery can also include **personification** and the use of **symbols** or **motifs**.

Try to comment on **other uses of language** such as parallel constructions and cumulative effects.

Don't just try and apply a checklist of techniques. Select the ones **most appropriate** for the piece under consideration.

The poem below is entitled *Birches* and was written by the American poet Robert Frost in the twentieth century.

When I see birches bend to left and right
Across the lines of straighter darker trees,
I like to think some boy's been swinging them.
But swinging doesn't bend them down to stay
As ice storms do. Often you must have seen them
Loaded with ice a sunny winter morning
After a rain. They click upon themselves
As the breeze rises, and turn many-colored
As the stir cracks and crazes their enamel.
Soon the sun's warmth makes them shed crystal shells
Shattering and avalanching on the snow crust –
Such heaps of broken glass to sweep away
You'd think the inner dome of heaven had fallen.
They are dragged to the withered bracken by the load,
And they seem not to break; though once they are bowed
So low for long, they never right themselves:
You may see their trunks arching in the woods
Years afterwards, trailing their leaves on the ground
Like girls on hands and knees that throw their hair
Before them over their heads to dry in the sun.
But I was going to say when Truth broke in
With all her matter of fact about the ice storm,
I should prefer to have some boy bend them
As he went out and in to fetch the cows –
Some boy too far from town to learn baseball,
Whose only play was what he found himself,
Summer or winter, and could play alone.
One by one he subdued his father's trees
By riding them down over and over again
Until he took the stiffness out of them,
And not one but hung limp, not one was left
For him to conquer. He learned all there was
To learn about not launching out too soon
And so not carrying the tree away
Clear to the ground, He always kept his poise
To the top branches, climbing carefully
With the same pains you use to fill a cup
Up to the brim, and even above the brim.
Then he flung outward, feet first, with a swish,
Kicking his way down through the air to the ground
So was I once myself a swinger of birches.
And so I dream of going back to be.
It's when I'm weary of considerations,
And life is too much like a pathless wood
Where your face burns and tickles with the cobwebs

Broken across it, and one eye is weeping
From a twig's having lashed across it open.
I'd like to get away from earth awhile
And then come back to it and begin over.
May no fate willfully misunderstand me
And half grant what I wish and snatch me away
Not to return. Earth's the right place for love:
I don't know where it's likely to go better.
I'd like to go by climbing a birch tree,
And climb black branches up a snow-white trunk
Toward heaven, till the tree could bear no more,
But dipped its top and set me down again.
That would be good both going and coming back.
One could do worse than be a swinger of birches.

Write a critical appreciation of the poem. In your answer your should consider:
• the use of voice in the poem;
• the use of language and description in the poem.

[Time allowed: 1 hour]

After writing your answer, turn to page 87 for help with marking it.

4 Drama

You will be expected to **analyse** and **comment** on extracts from different types of play from different periods.

There are a number of possible questions you may be presented with. For example, you may be asked to discuss the **dramatic presentation** of a particular character or theme; you may be asked to explore the way **dramatic tension** is created; you may be asked to consider the **use of setting**.

You will be encouraged to examine the **use of language** itself within the context of drama; how it contributes to our understanding of characters, moods and ideas.

Typical Exam Question

The passage below appears in *Hamlet*, written by William Shakespeare.

In it, the King, Claudius, at his first public meeting, tries to persuade his nephew that he should stop mourning the death of his father, the previous king. Hamlet, however, suspects that his uncle has murdered his father. He also resents the way that his mother, the Queen, married his uncle so soon after his father's death. She, although apparently unaware of how Claudius has acquired power, supports his attempts to persuade Hamlet to change his outlook and attitude.

KING: But now, my cousin Hamlet, and my son –

HAMLET: [*Aside*] A little more than kin, and less than kind.

KING: How is it that the clouds still hang on you?

HAMLET: Not so, my lord; I am too much in the sun.

QUEEN: Good Hamlet, cast thy nighted colour off,
              And let thine eye look like a friend on Denmark.
              Do not for ever with thy vailed lids
              Seek for thy noble father in the dust.
              Thou know'st 'tis common – all that lives must die
              Passing through nature to eternity.

HAMLET: Ay, madam, it is common.

QUEEN: If it be,
              Why seems it so particular with thee?

HAMLET: Seems, madam! Nay, it is; I know not seems.
         'Tis not alone my inky cloak, good mother,
         Nor customary suits of solemn black,
         Nor windy suspiration of forc'd breath,
         No, nor the fruitful river in the eye,
         Nor the dejected haviour of the visage,
         Together with all forms, moods, shapes of grief,
         That can denote me truly. These, indeed, seem;
         For they are actions that a man might play;
         But I have that within which passes show –
         These but the trappings and the suits of woe.

KING: 'Tis sweet and commendable in your nature, Hamlet,
         To give these mourning duties to your father;
         But you must know your father lost a father;
         That father lost lost his; and the survivor bound,
         In filial obligation, for some term
         To do obsequious Sorrow. But to persever
         In obstinate condolement is a course
         Of impious stubbornness; 'tis unmanly grief;
         It shows a will most incorrect to heaven,
         A heart unfortified, a mind impatient,
         An understanding simple and unschool'd;
         For what we know must be, and is as common
         As any the most vulgar thing to sense,
         Why should we in our peevish opposition
         Take it to heart? Fie! 'tis a fault to heaven,
         A fault against the dead, a fault to nature,
         To reason most absurd; whose common theme
         Is death of fathers, and who still hath cried,
         From the first corse till he that died to-day,
         'This must be so'.

Consider the presentation of the characters of Hamlet and the King here. In your answer you should:
• assess how the dramatic situation shapes their behaviour;
• comment on each character's use of language.

[Time allowed: 1 hour]

How to tackle this question

You should not rush into your answer. Plan your work. Don't be afraid to <u>highlight</u> key words and phrases on the question paper itself.

Explore the extract in **sections**, looking for **similarities** and **differences** between them. This will allow you to study the **progression** of the passage.

Consider some of these further points before you begin writing:

- In drama characters are often putting on **appearances** in front of others. Sometimes the other characters are **aware** of this and sometimes they are not. Often the audience is fully aware of the role-playing going on.

- This **role-playing** often creates an **underlying tension** or **dramatic conflict**. In other words, there is a **hidden layer** or **subtext** within the words being spoken. For example, here Claudius and Hamlet are, in a way, testing each other out beneath their public words. Sometimes a **character** – here the Queen – **seems unaware** of what is **really** going on.

- How is language used to create this **hidden tension**? You should consider who is speaking to whom and what **methods they use to express themselves**. For example, Claudius appears to **compliment** and **flatter** his nephew in a very polite controlled and accommodating way; at the same time he is aware that Hamlet speaks more to his mother than him, and that he talks in an emotional manner with **hidden implications**.

- Look at the **images** that characters use to express their ideas. **Images** include **descriptive language**, **metaphors** and **similes**. A **metaphor** is a direct comparison which is not literally true ('He is a tiger'). A **simile** is also a comparison, using **'like'** or **'as'**, which is also literally not real ('She looks like a statue'). The important thing about metaphors and similes is to **explore what ideas or qualities they bring to mind and what they tell us about the speaker and his/her view of other characters and events**. For example, in the extract the King tells Hamlet that 'the clouds still hang on' his nephew. This is not literally true. It tells us that from Claudius's point of view his nephew seems gloomy and in a dark mood. It is the dark mood that Claudius wishes to explore, to see if Hamlet has an ulterior motive for his gloom, a possible suspicion of what he himself has done to achieve power.

- Are there any **similar types of images** that seem to appear? Can you see any similar patterns of comparisons or any **contrasting patterns**? Why might these be there? Do they **echo** or **reflect** any key **themes** or **ideas**?

- Study the way characters **shape their words and phrases**. Look at the **syntax** of sections of their speeches, the **order** in which words and phrases are delivered. Do they speak in **short sequences**? Do they use **repeated kinds of constructions**? Do they use **balanced phrases**? Short sequences may indicate a reluctance to communicate, a hidden purpose. Repeated kinds of construction can indicate emphatic emotion as in Hamlet's long speech in the extract or they can suggest control and balance such as when the King tries to remind Hamlet that all fathers die. Balanced phrases often rely on the use of a **caesura** (a line which can be seen as consisting of equal halves weighted by punctuation – such as the King's use of 'A heart unfortified, a mind impatient') and can imply that the character is in control, logical and rational.

Extracts from a Grade C answer

GOOD POINTS

Reeta has tried to address the first part of the question and explore the **dramatic situation**. She has sensed that both characters are putting on an **act** and has noted how the King is aware he is being watched by the rest of the court.

She has offered some comment on how the characters **address** each other, such as the King complimenting Hamlet who, in turn speaks an aside and then in a seeming riddle.

Reeta has understood that there is a **hidden tension** or **subtext** in the way that Hamlet seems to pose a threat to the listening King. She has also noted that Claudius is in a difficult position and the **dramatic situation** prevents him from responding openly to his nephew's words.

She has shown **understanding** of Claudius's final speech, his apparent advice to Hamlet and the way in which he tries to control his language whilst resisting any provocation from his nephew.

At the beginning of the extract the King seems to show care and concern for Hamlet in the way that he calls him his 'son'. Hamlet seems unwilling to accept the compliment as he speaks words under his breath rather than replying directly to the King. Claudius is aware that the rest of the court is watching so he keeps his temper and tries to ask his question in a considerate way, putting on an act for the audience. Hamlet again refuses to participate in this charade and replies in words which seem like a riddle. In fact he seems to address his mother rather than the King and speaks in a passionate way to her. We can tell this by the use of the exclamation mark in 'Seems, madam!' His words may not mean much to the innocent Queen but may convey a threat to Claudius when he speaks about 'I have that within which passes show', implying he knows more than he is saying; he is putting on an act too just as Claudius is in this scene.

The King is careful not to be provoked by Hamlet's words and carries on talking to him like a father addressing a young child. He tries to offer him worldly advice and tells him that it is a natural cycle, that all things live and die. He tries to make him 'grow up' by telling Hamlet he is being 'unmanly'. He tries to suggest that Hamlet is offending God by his obstinate mourning...

40

How to score higher marks

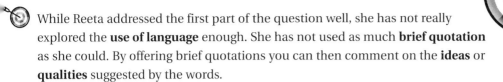

○ While Reeta addressed the first part of the question well, she has not really explored the **use of language** enough. She has not used as much **brief quotation** as she could. By offering brief quotations you can then comment on the **ideas** or **qualities** suggested by the words.

○ Reeta could have explored some of the **images** or **patterns of words** in the text. There is a **pattern** of darkness and covering up; words like 'clouds', 'nighted colour', 'vailed' and 'suits of solemn black' convey the idea of gloom but also of surface appearances, of something closed and concealed. They **echo** the **idea** that Claudius and Hamlet are putting on an act and hiding their true motives and feelings.

○ Reeta could have explored the **syntax** in certain sequences more to consider its **purpose** or **effect**. For example, Claudius's opening speech seems, on the surface, to be considerate and caring; yet he calls Hamlet his 'cousin' first and then his 'son' almost as an afterthought; the **subtext** could be that the King is not that fatherly after all.

○ There is also the opportunity to examine the **progression** of the passage. Reeta works through the sequence but has not really looked for **differences** and **similarities** between sections in terms of **imagery**, **constructions** and **phrasing**. For example, Hamlet's speech to the Queen contains the use of **repeated constructions** ('Nor...') and a kind of exhaustive listing technique ('forms, moods, shapes of grief') to express the enormity of his feelings. In a similar way, the King's final speech also contains the use of **repeated constructions and phrases** ('you rather lost a father;/That father lost lost his') but here the effort is to sound logical and reasoned, not emotional. There is less use of **imagery** in this section of the extract as Claudius tries to sound wise and practical in his approach.

Typical Exam Question

The passage below is taken from *A Streetcar Named Desire*, by Tennessee Williams. In it, Blanche Dubois, who has been forced by circumstances to move from the American South to live with her sister, Stella, and brother-in-law, Stanley, talks about her past and romance.

STANLEY: What does it cost for a string of fur-pieces like that?

BLANCHE: Why, those were a tribute from an admirer of mine!

STANLEY: He must have had a lot of – admiration!

BLANCHE: Oh, in my youth I excited some admiration. But look at me now! [*She smiles at him radiantly*] Would you think it possible that I was once considered to be – attractive?

STANLEY: Your looks are okay.

BLANCHE: I was fishing for a compliment, Stanley.

STANLEY: I don't go in for that stuff.

BLANCHE: What – stuff?

STANLEY: Compliments to women about their looks. I never met a woman that didn't know if she was good-looking or not without being told, and some of them give themselves credit for more than they've got. I once went out with a doll who said to me, 'I am the glamorous type, I am the glamorous type!' I said, 'So what?'

BLANCHE: And what did she say then?

STANLEY: She didn't say nothing. That shut her up like a clam.

BLANCHE: Did it end the romance?

STANLEY: It ended the conversation – that was all. Some men are took in by this Hollywood glamour stuff and some men are not.

BLANCHE: I'm sure you belong to the second category.

STANLEY: That's right.

BLANCHE: I cannot imagine any witch of a woman casting a spell over you.

STANLEY: That's – right.

BLANCHE: You're simple, straightforward and honest, a little bit on the primitive side I should think. To interest you a woman would have to – [*She pauses with an indefinite gesture.*]

STANLEY [*slowly*]: Lay... her cards on the table.

BLANCHE [*smiling*]: Yes – yes – cards on the table. ... Well, life is too full of evasions and ambiguities, I think. I like an artist who paints in strong, bold colours, primary colours. I don't like pinks and creams and I never cared for wish-washy people. That was why, when you walked in here last night, I said to myself – 'My sister has married a man!' – Of course that was all that I could tell about you.

STANLEY [*booming*]: Now let's cut the re-bop!

BLANCHE [*pressing hands to her ears*]: Ouuuuu!

STELLA [*calling from the steps*]: Stanley! You come out here and let Blanche finish dressing!

BLANCHE: I'm through dressing, honey.

STELLA: Well, you come out, then.

STANLEY: Your sister and I are having a little talk.

BLANCHE [*lightly*]: Honey, do me a favour. Run to the drug-store and get me a lemon-coke with plenty of chipped ice in it! – Will you do that for me, Sweetie?

STELLA [*uncertainly*]: Yes. [*She goes round the corner of the building.*]

BLANCHE: The poor thing was out there listening to us, and I have an idea she doesn't understand you as well as I do... All right; now, Mr Kowalski, let us proceed without any more double-talk. I'm ready to answer all questions. I've nothing to hide. What is it?

Comment on the presentation of Blanche and Stanley here. In your answer you should:
• comment on the interaction between the characters;
• consider their use of language.

[Time allowed: 1 hour]

How to tackle this question

● Remember to look at the passage in **sections**, looking for **similarities** and **differences** between them so that you can offer comments on the **progression** of the extract. For example, keep an eye on who is **controlling the dialogue** here. Is it one character or does it alternate between them? How is this achieved?

● See if there is any sense of any of the characters **role-playing** here. We saw in the extract from *Hamlet* that two of the three characters seemed to be putting on an act of some kind to conceal some hidden motive. It may well be that only one character in a scene is putting on a role and that role-playing lies in sharp contrast to another character who is being completely natural and open about his or her thoughts and feelings.

● Look at the ways in which characters **address** each other. Are they flattering, insulting? Do the characters **express their thoughts openly** or **in hidden ways** as Hamlet did?

● Does the passage have any **imagery** or **patterns of words**?

● Look for the use of **register** in this kind of dialogue, the **styles of speech** that different characters may use. The **contrasts between differing registers** may develop the **hidden tension** or **dramatic conflict** beneath the surface.

There is a clear contrast between the two protagonists here, not only in the way they speak and their attitudes but in the hidden and unspoken tension beneath the surface. Stanley addresses Blanche at the beginning in a direct and off-hand fashion with his initial question, his main concern apparent in the word 'cost'. It is the material aspect which interests him. His blunt and unadorned language is reinforced by his direct refusal to play flirting games with Blanche: 'I don't go in for that stuff'. His speeches tend to be spoken in brief assertive short sequences: 'She didn't say nothing...It ended the conversation....That's right'. He is testing his sister-in-law, probing her motives, trying to speak man to man: 'Now let's cut the re-bop'. The register of his language is down to earth, street wise and plain; he went out 'with a doll' and 'That shut her up like a clam'. There is a force and brutality in his direct statements which will not be put off by any fancy talking; his language conveys his physical presence and no nonsense opinions.

On the other hand, Blanche tries to counter this presence by acting coyly and flirtatiously, offering feminine attitudes and a sense of delicacy; at the same time she is attempting to convey her apparent superior knowledge and status in comparison to the lowly Stanley. She adopts words like 'admirer' instead of 'lover'; she looks for compliments that are not forthcoming, trying to delay her inquisitor's probing of her background and reasons for being in the household. She tries to keep on his good side by feeding him compliments: 'I cannot imagine any witch of a woman casting a spell over you.'. She keeps her language formal and correct, even addressing him as 'Mr Kowalski'. She cannot avoid trying to put him down though: 'You're simple, straightforward and honest, a little bit on the primitive side...' In trying to control the direction of the conversation she is only antagonising her potential enemy more. The opposition increases as she tries to offer him romantic philosophy and delicate words: 'I like an artist who paints in strong, bold colours, primary colours. I don't like pinks and creams and I never cared for wishy-washy people'. Her attempts to flatter and control him again do not have the desired effect.

The idea of Blanche's pretence, her frail and romantic exterior, is echoed in the way she addresses her sister as 'honey' and 'sweetie'. It appears sincere but to Stanley only adds to the condescending atmosphere he is in. At the close Blanche seems to confirm the act she has been adapting when she claims there will be no 'more double-talk'; in fact most of the double-talk has emerged from her. She has relinquished temporary control...

Why this scores high marks

Luke has produced a promising high level response. He has managed to convey a sense of the **progression** of the passage as well as a sense of the **hidden tension** beneath the surface.

He has grasped the **contrast** between the **act** of Blanche and the **natural** and **brutal** approach of Stanley.

He has commented on how the characters **address each other** and their different uses of **constructions** and **register**. He has noted that the different characters express their thoughts in open or more closed ways depending on their motives.

He has explored the **interaction between characters** and who is **controlling the dialogue** at different stages. He has managed to touch upon the different **attitudes** of the characters.

Don't forget ...

Break the extract into **sections** before you begin so that you can look for **similarities** and **differences** between them. This will allow you to study the **progression** of the passage.

Look for **contrasts** between **characters** in terms of their **attitudes** and **motives**.

See if one or more of the characters is **putting on an act** of some kind and consider the reasons **why**.

Look out for examples of **imagery** and **patterns of similar or contrasting words**. Consider the **ideas** and **qualities** they suggest and what they tell us about the **speaker** who uses them. Do they echo or reflect **ideas** or **themes**?

Look for the use of **syntax** (the order in which ideas are expressed), **repeated constructions** and **balanced phrases**. Do they convey emotion or rational thought?

Look for the use of different **registers** (styles of language) and what they tell us about the status and motives of the characters.

The passage below comes from *Waiting for Godot*, by Samuel Beckett. In it, two tramps, Vladimir and Estragon, occupy their time while waiting, as they do day after day in the same place, for the arrival of Godot.

VLADIMIR: Show your leg.

ESTRAGON: Which?

VLADIMIR: Both. Pull up your trousers. [*Estragon gives a leg to Vladimir, staggers.Vladimir takes the leg. They stagger.*] Pull up your trousers.

ESTRAGON: I can't.

[*Vladimir pulls up the trousers, looks at the leg, lets it go. Estragon almost falls.*]
VLADIMIR : The other. [*Estragon gives the same leg.*] The other, pig! [*Estragon gives the other leg. Triumphantly*] There's the wound! Beginning to fester!

ESTRAGON: And what about it?

VLADIMIR: [*letting go the leg.*] Where are your boots?

ESTRAGON: I must have thrown them away.

VLADIMIR: When?

ESTRAGON: I don't know.

VLADIMIR: Why?

ESTRAGON: [*exasperated.*] I don't know why I don't know!

VLADIMIR: No, I mean why did you throw them away?

ESTRAGON: [*exasperated.*] Because they were hurting me!

VLADIMIR: [*triumphantly pointing to the boots.*] There they are! [*Estragon looks at the boots.*] At the very spot where you left them yesterday!

[*Estragon goes towards the boots, inspects them closely.*]
ESTRAGON: They're not mine.

VLADIMIR: [*stupefied.*] Not yours!

ESTRAGON: Mine were black. These are brown.

VLADIMIR: You're sure yours were black?

ESTRAGON: Well, they were a kind of grey.

VLADIMIR: And these are brown? Show.

ESTRAGON: [*picking up a boot*]. Well, they're a kind of green.

VLADIMIR: Show. [*Estragon hands him the boot. Vladimir inspects it, throws it down angrily*] Well of all the –

ESTRAGON: You see, all that's a lot of bloody –

VLADIMIR: Ah! I see what it is. Yes, I see what's happened.

ESTRAGON: All that's a lot of bloody –

VLADIMIR: It's elementary. Someone came and took yours and left you his.

ESTRAGON: Why?

VLADIMIR: His were too tight for him, so he took yours.

ESTRAGON: But mine were too tight.

VLADIMIR: For you. Not for him.

ESTRAGON: [*having tried in vain to work it out.*] I'm tired! [*Pause.*] Let's go.

VLADIMIR: We can't.

ESTRAGON: Why not?

VLADIMIR: We're waiting for Godot.

ESTRAGON: Ah! [*Pause. Despairing.*] What'll we do, what'll we do!

VLADIMIR: There's nothing we can do.

ESTRAGON: But I can't go on like this!

VLADIMIR: Would you like a radish?

Consider the presentation of Vladimir and Estragon here. In your answer you should explore:
• the relationship of the characters;
• their use of language.

[Time allowed: 1 hour]

After writing your answer, turn to page 88 for help with marking it.

5 Speech and dialogue

You will be assessed on your ability to **analyse** and **comment** on extracts from different kinds of speech or dialogue.

You may be expected to comment on transcripts of **natural spontaneous speech**; to explore the techniques used in different forms of **scripted speech**; and to discuss how **fictional dialogue** is constructed.

You may also be required to **compare** these different forms of spoken language.

Typical Exam Question

Passage A below is a transcript from a conversation in which a great-uncle describes some of the experiences of his youth to other members of his family. The speaker comes from Norfolk.

Passage B is an extract from *Two on a Tower*, a novel by Thomas Hardy. In the passage the parson attempts to train members of a small rural community in Wessex (a fictional area based on the countryside of Southern England) to sing as a choir.

Passage A

The following key can be used as a guide:

Note: (.)   = micro pause

    (1) (2) = pauses in seconds

    -        = emphatic stress of words

Well (.) you know I was in the band (.) St Faith's band you know (.) well we went a-carol-playing there one (.) just before Christmas (2) we went all round St Faith's and Newton St Faith's (.) and then we went up to the Manor (3) and there was a lot a mud up that old loke and ol' Jack Fisher said (.) i.i.i. ah.h o.o.o. w.wor what about the m.mud (.) he said (.) I g.got some w.water boots on b.but they g.got a h.hole in the bottom (1) course ol' Jack used to stutter you see (.) anyway, we kept agoing 'n' they called at the King's Head and that got on there 'til past ten and so they said (.) well we'd better (.) have one more tune before we go home (1) so they played a carol or one or two carols round there (.) 'til someone said (.) you know what you are doing altogether don't ya (2) what someone said (.) you're playing to an old haystack (.) huh they said (.) that was a wrong un (.) so we had to pack that up (.) and of course we had to go home cos some of them weren't feeling too good (.) it was dark you know (.) and we didn't know where we were.

Passage B

The parson announced psalm fifty-third to the tune of 'Devizes', and his voice burst forth with

> 'The Lord look'd down from Heav'n's high tower
> The sons of men to view',

in notes of rigid cheerfulness.

In this start, however, he was joined only by the girls and boys, the men furnishing but an accompaniment of ahas and hems. Mr Torkingham stopped, and Sammy Blore spoke, – 'Beg your pardon, sir, – if you'll deal mild with us a moment. What with the wind and walking, my throat's as rough as a grater; and not knowing you were going to hit up[1] that minute, I hadn't hawked,[2] and I don't think Hezzy and Nat had, either, – had ye, souls?'

'I hadn't got thorough ready, that's true,' said Hezekiah.

'Quite right of you, then, to speak,' said Mr Torkingham. 'Don't mind explaining; we are here for practice. Now clear your throats, then, and at it again.'

There was a noise as of atmospheric hoes and scrapers, and the bass contingent at last got under way with a time of its own:

'The Lard looked down vrom Heav'n's high tower!'

'Ah, that's where we are so defective – the pronunciation,' interrupted the parson. 'Now repeat after me: "The Lord look'd down from Heav'n's high tower."'
The choir repeated like an exaggerative echo: 'The Lawd look'd daown from Heav'n's high towah!'

'Better!' said the parson, in the strenuously sanguine tones of a man who got his living by discovering a bright side in things where it was not very perceptible to other people. 'But it should not be given with quite so extreme an accent; or we may be called affected by other parishes. And, Nathaniel Chapman, there's a jauntiness in your manner of singing which is not quite becoming. Why don't you sing more earnestly?'

'My conscience won't let me, sir. They say every man for himself: but, thank God, I'm not so mean as to lessen old fokes' chances by being earnest at my time o' life, and they so much nearer the need o't.'

[1] hit up: start singing.

[2] hawked: cleared throat

Compare the extracts paying particular attention to:

• the speakers' vocabulary and expression;

• the differences between natural and fictional speech.

[Time allowed: 1 hour]

How to tackle this question

Don't rush into your answer but plan your work. Don't be afraid to **highlight** key words and phrases on the question paper itself.

Explore the extract in **sections**, looking for **similarities** and **differences** between them. This will allow you to study the **progression** of the passage.

Consider these further points before you begin writing:

- There are a number of things to consider and select from when considering a transcript of **natural spontaneous speech**. <u>Don't</u> just try and apply a checklist of techniques without seeing, firstly, whether they are relevant to the extract and, secondly, how they contribute to our understanding of the speaker's mood, beliefs and attitudes.

- You should consider the **use of pauses**, **fillers** and **phatic communication** (features which are ordinary expressions but do not really contribute to the expression of ideas). These elements are clear indications of unrehearsed speech, showing the speaker taking time to think or to gauge a response.

- Look at any **contextual information** given and try to assess who the speaker is talking to.

- Look at **pronunciation** and the use of particular **stresses** or **rises and falls in pitch**. Try to consider why these happen and their effects on the speaker's meaning.

- Try to comment on the speaker's **vocabulary**. Does it seem to be part of the **dialect**? What is the effect on our **understanding**?

- When considering **fictional dialogue**, try to see if the author has used any methods to show pauses or fillers.

- When assessing **fictional dialogue**, try to see how the writer has conveyed the ideas of **dialect** and **accent**. Has phonetic spelling been used? Are there certain words or phrases which seem to indicate the speaker comes from a particular place or region?

- In the same way, **compare how different characters speak** in the passage. Do they all talk in the same way? Do some have a regional dialect and vocabulary? Do some speak in received pronunciation (the idea of a form of Standard English which essentially lacks an accent and follows 'correct' rules of pronunciation, grammar and expression). If there are **contrasts** (a technique discussed in the chapters on Drama and Poetry) what kinds of **attitudes and values** are suggested by the characters? Do some of the talkers seem more or less educated, more authoritative, to have more prestige?

GOOD POINTS

Julie shows that she is aware of some of the differences between natural and constructed fictional speech.

She has shown a clear awareness of some of the devices used in spontaneous speech such as the use of fillers, pauses and qualifying statements. Julie has also detected the relaxed style of delivery and the speaker's awareness of his audience.

She has demonstrated awareness of pronunciation and dialect, commenting on vowel sounds and aspects of vocabulary to some effect.

Julie has also suggested that in the fictional dialogue the author has perhaps invented or highlighted particular words and phrases to suggest the speakers' origins. Julie has successfully made an effective comparison between the use of vowel sounds in both passages and the way that in the second extract this has been achieved through the use of phonetic spelling.

She has also begun to see the possible use of contrast between the way the parson speaks in relation to the way the members of the choir address him.

The speaker in Passage A uses a lot of fillers such as 'you know' and 'anyway' which seem to show he is thinking as he is speaking. This is also shown by the way that he pauses every so often. He also qualifies his statements which interrupts the flow of his story, as if he wishes his listeners to pick up all the fine details: 'so they played a carol or one or two carols...' We can see that it is an informal conversation; he seems quite relaxed with his audience and uses contractions like "til' and "n'. There seem to be words specific to the region he comes from in the way that they are used or pronounced. He likes to use the word "ol' before mentioning Jack Fisher as he repeats it twice, possibly as a sign of respect or affection. He employs words like 'loke' for lake suggesting that the vowel sounds he makes are not those of Standard English. He also uses words which seem to join standard words together to give a flavour of his dialect; for example, like 'agoing'.

Passage B is clearly not spontaneous speech. Hardy has given his characters a particular vocabulary to indicate that they come from a particular region. They use words like 'hawked' and 'hit up'. There is also the use of phonetic spelling to show that the speakers also have vowel sounds that do not echo those of Standard English. For example, they say things like 'The Lard' and 'The Lawd', as if they are unable to imitate the sounds the parson is trying to get them to copy.

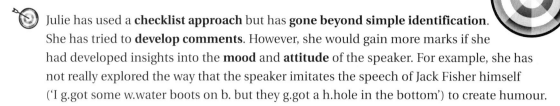

Julie has used a **checklist approach** but has **gone beyond simple identification**. She has tried to **develop comments**. However, she would gain more marks if she had developed insights into the **mood** and **attitude** of the speaker. For example, she has not really explored the way that the speaker imitates the speech of Jack Fisher himself ('I g.got some w.water boots on b. but they g.got a h.hole in the bottom') to create humour.

Similarly she could explore further the use of the speaker's **use of stress** to create humour. For example, he tries to convey the absurdity of their situation by emphasising the word 'haystack' and at the close of the passage we can imagine his voice rising as he stresses that the band 'didn't know <u>where</u> we were'.

When considering the **fictional dialogue**, Julie seems less confident. She has noticed aspects of **vocabulary** and **pronunciation** but could develop the contrast between Mr Torkingham and the members of the choir in much more depth. He tends to speak in received pronunciation using formal expression and vocabulary. This would seem to indicate a form of authority and prestige on behalf of the speaker in comparison to the seemingly less educated members of the choir. There are also possible issues of class here too.

Julie could also consider the role of the **authorial voice** here. This is a form of control and intervention not used in the transcript of natural speech and conveys **further attitudes and mood**. Whereas the **humour** in Passage A arises from the speaker himself, it arises here through the author's control and intervention. His description of 'the strenuously sanguine tones of a man who got his living by discovering a bright side in things where it was not very perceptible' underlines the parson's polite and humorous efforts to communicate with the choir.

Julie could also have spotted how the writer is unable to convey **pauses and fillers** as expressed in the transcript of natural speech. In Passage B Hardy indicates these by describing how there was an 'accompaniment of ahas and hems'.

The passage below is an extract from a speech given by the Native American Chief Seattle to the American President in 1854. In it he describes the attitudes of his people towards nature and the environment compared to those of other Americans.

How can you buy or sell the sky, the warmth of the land? The idea is strange to us.

If we do not own the freshness of the air and the sparkle of the water, how can you buy them?

Every part of this earth is sacred to my people.

Every shining pine needle, every sandy shore, every mist in the dark woods, every clearing and humming insect is holy in the memory and experience of my people. The sap which courses through the trees carried the memories of the red man.

The white man's dead forget the country of their birth when they go to walk among the stars. Our dead never forget this beautiful earth, for it is the mother of the red man.

We are part of the earth and it is part of us. The perfumed flowers are our sisters; the deer, the horse, the great eagle, these are our brothers.

The rocky crests, the juices in the meadows, the body heat of the pony, and man – all belong to the same family.

So, when the Great Chief in Washington sends word that he wishes to buy our land, he asks much of us. The Great Chief sends word he will reserve us a place so that we can live comfortably to ourselves.

He will be our father and we will be his children. So we will consider your offer to buy our land.

But it will not be easy. For this land is sacred to us.

This shining water that moves in the streams and rivers is not just water but the blood of our ancestors.

If we sell you land, you must remember that it is sacred, and you must teach your children that it is sacred and that each ghostly reflection in the clear water of the lakes tells of events and memories in the life of my people.

The water's murmur is the voice of my father's father.

The rivers are our brothers, they quench our thirst. The rivers carry our canoes, and feed our children. If we sell you our land, you must remember, and teach your children, that the rivers are our brothers, and yours, and you must henceforth give the rivers the kindness you would give any brother.

We know that the white man does not understand our ways. One portion of land is the same to him as the next, for he is a stranger who comes in the night and takes from the land whatever he needs.

The earth is not his brother; but his enemy, and when he has conquered it, he moves on.

He leaves his father's graves behind, and he does not care. He kidnaps the earth from his children, and he does not care.

His father's grave and his children's birthright, are forgotten. He treats his mother; the earth, and his brother; the sky, as things to be bought, plundered, sold like sheep or bright beads.

His appetite will devour the earth and leave behind only a desert.

I do not know. Our ways are different from your ways.

Write a critical appreciation of this speech. In your answer you should:
• comment on the speaker's vocabulary and expression;
• the techniques the speaker uses to try and persuade his audience.

[Time allowed: 1 hour]

How to tackle this question

- Remember that this is not a transcript of natural spontaneous speech. It has been written down and crafted to achieve certain effects and is there to **persuade** the listeners.

- Remember to **highlight key words and phrases** and to **divide** the passage into **smaller sections** so you can look for **similarities** and **differences** between them.

- Assess the **audience** for the speech, **its context** and its **purpose**.

- Consider whether the speaker uses **contrasts** in any specific way, as discussed in previous chapters.

- Consider the speaker's use of **vocabulary**. Is **imagery** used in any way? Can you notice the use of any **patterns** or **contrasts** in the imagery?

- Examine the **rhetorical devices** the speaker employs. Are **questions** used in a particular way?

- Look at the speaker's **phrasing**. Are balanced phrases, cumulative effects, lists of three, repetition and syntax used for any particular purposes?

The speaker here is not really making a protest but offering a thoughtful speech comparing two different outlooks and philosophies. His ideas are based on the contrasts between different ways of life. His words offer a formal note of regret and resignation that this is the way things are. His speech opens with a question, using carefully balanced phrasing: 'How can you buy or sell the sky, the warmth of the land?' His sense of measured poise is reflected in the structure and the way he selects his vocabulary indicates his bemusement at the Americans' approach to life; the notion of buying something abstract, something which is not owned by anyone — the sky — confirms his uncertainty. He opposes his use of questions with brief and assertive statements about the attitudes and beliefs of his 'people': he confirms their difference ('The idea is strange to us') and uses repeated phrasing to convey the idea that belief in the land is a central tenet of their religion — 'Every part of the earth is sacred to my people...Every'.

He then uses a cumulative technique of detailing precise examples of the land to intimate that even the most minute object has a spiritual and not a material value as it does for other Americans: 'shining pine needle, every sandy shore, every mist in the dark woods...' The Chief is careful to return to some of his key ideas and phrases later in his speech when he echoes his earlier idea that 'this land is sacred to us'. His ideas revolve around this concept of faith and his language draws on images which refer to the heavens and the earth to reinforce the idea that life and spirit are all embracing; he refers to the 'sky' and 'the stars', yet at the same time he describes 'the rocky crests, the juices in the meadows'. Both high and low, the material and the abstract are linked by a living force of life and the Chief emphasises this by his reference to 'the sap which courses through the trees' and how the 'shining water' contains 'the blood of' his 'ancestors'. There is a bond, a force, which not only unites the sky and the earth but the native Americans, their environment, both their past and present members.

The land and sky are their living history and are personified as 'all' belonging 'to the same family'.

The notion that the elements of Nature and humanity are inextricably linked into a family leads the Chief to describe the earth as the 'mother of the red man'; the President has now become 'our father and we will be his children'. Yet the Chief develops this comparison by reminding the President that 'The water's murmur is the voice of my father's father' and that 'The rivers are our brothers', as if to say that his real 'family' will always be found in the elements not in the President's control and patronage. He is again asserting his and his people's difference to other Americans in a gentle and non-provocative manner...

Why this scores high marks

- David has produced a promising high level response that offers an awareness of **progression** and blends detailed comments on ideas with a sharp awareness of some of the techniques used to express them.

- David has clearly addressed the ideas of **audience**, **context** and **purpose** at the beginning of his answer and has commented on the mood behind the speaker's intentions.

- He has explored ideas of **contrast** and built his answer around them.

- David has commented on contrasting **patterns of imagery** and sensed how the speaker uses **personification** to develop his meaning and beliefs.

- David has also been aware of **other uses of language** such as the speaker's use of **phrasing**, cumulative effects, parallel constructions, repetition of key words and phrases and the use of questions. He has not simply identified these but has commented on their effects and how they are used.

Don't forget ...

Remember to **highlight key words and phrases** and to **divide** the passage into **smaller sections** so you can look for **similarities** and **differences**.

Look at the **audience**, **purpose** and **context** of the speech or dialogue.

See if there is any use of **contrast** in terms of ideas or the way different speakers use or deliver language.

Look at the speaker's **vocabulary** and at any **patterns of imagery**.

Explore the speaker's use of **pronunciation** and **stress**. What do they contribute to our understanding?

Look at other uses of language such as **rhetorical devices** (to persuade or influence), **phrasing** and **syntax**. What do they contribute to our understanding?

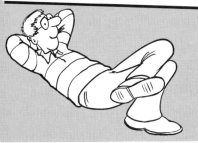

Don't simply try and apply a checklist. Comment on the **mood**, **attitudes**, **beliefs** and **status** of the speaker.

Question to try

Passage A below is a transcript of a real interview with a woman from Gloucestershire in which she speaks about her work.

Passage B is taken from *Under the Greenwood Tree*, a novel by Thomas Hardy. The speakers live in the fictional world of Wessex and speak with a country accent. In the passage Reuben Dewy, a tranter (a kind of travelling salesman), and his wife discuss his appearance.

Passage A

Note: [.] indicates a brief pause. The interviewer's questions are not transcribed. A key to symbols used to indicate stress and intonation is given at the end of the transcript.

well for a start call me Ame [.] everybody else do. I'm the only one [.] in the whole of Gloucestershire [.] after twenty six year [.] nineteen thirty nine when war broke out I seed the advertisement in the newspaper [.] and our dad said to I well he said if thee carns't do that as good as some of the men he said that's a poor job [.] well I thought myself well I wouldn't let the old man down so I had a go [.] that's nineteen thirty nine [.] and I'm still going strong...

well it was on account of the money [.] they was paying [.] they was paying more – or an hour than what I was getting where I [.] was before... all sorts sk.. It's [.] it's got grass-cutting to do [.] in the winter put down the grit [.] it's got siding [.] channelling [.] I've even put up signposts.. even put up signposts...

no[.] I er I'm classed as a roadworker [.] I do all the jobs all [.] all but the manual labour which is carried out by the men... all round Hutton [.] Coombe [.] Sinnel [.] Blackwaters and er all round Worlds End Lane and up Sinnel Lane again and that's my worst piece on my area is Sinnel Lane [.] all the fish and chip paper is chucked up the bank and the kids is on the top of the lane scorting the bloody stones down [.] and it ain't a bit of good to sweep it up because it's just as bad in ten minutes after...

they do [.] and it ain't no good to have litter baskets. ..not a bit of good [.] and it ain't no good to tell them [.] cos they'll say all right to thee face and behind thee back there's [.] b. and we's just as bad as ever.. well [.] take them on the average and they been't too bad [.] but still there's [.] there's ways [.] and way [.] means for improvement...

oh toffee papers sweet papers lollipops [.] there's sticks [.] all the ruddy lot... all on it [.] you can get barrowfuls...

Passage B

'Really, Reuben; 'tis quite a disgrace to see such a man,' said Mrs. Dewy (with the severity justifiable in a long-tried companion), giving him another turn round and picking several of Smiler's hairs from the shoulder of his coat. Reuben's thoughts seemed engaged elsewhere, and he yawned. 'And the collar of your coat is a shame to behold – so plastered with dirt, or dust, or grease, or something. Why, wherever could you have got it?'

''Tis my warm nater in summer-time, I suppose. I always did get in such a heat when I bustle about.'

'Ay, the Dewys always were such a coarse-skinned family. There's your brother Bob just as bad – as fat as a porpoise – wi' his low, mean, "How'st do, Ann?" whenever he meets me. I'd "How'st do" him indeed! If the sun only shines out a minute, there be you all streaming in the face, I never see!'

'If I be hot week-days I must be hot Sundays.'

'If any of the girls should turn after their father 'twill be a bad look-out for 'em, poor things. None of my family was sich vulgar sweaters – not one of 'em. But Lord-a-mercy – the Dewys! I don't know how ever I cam' into such a family.'

'Your woman's weakness when I asked ye to jine us – that's how it was, I suppose.' But the tranter appeared to have heard some such words from his wife before, and hence his answer had not the energy it might have shown if the enquiry had possessed the charm of novelty.

'You never did look so well in a pair of trousers as in them,' she continued in the same unimpassioned voice, so that the unfriendly criticism of the Dewy family seemed to have been more normal than spontaneous. 'Such a cheap pair as 'twas, too. As big as any man could wish to have, and lined inside and double-lined in the lower parts, and an extra piece of stiffening at the bottom. And 'tis a nice high cut that comes up right under your armpits, and there's enough turned down inside the seams to make half a pair more, besides a piece of cloth left that will make an honest waistcoat: all by my contriving in buying the stuff at a bargain and having it made up under my eye. It only shows what may be done by taking a little trouble and not going straight to the rascally tailors.'

Compare the extracts, paying particular attention to:

• the speakers' vocabulary and expression;
• the differences between natural and fictional speech.

[Time allowed: 1 hour]

After writing your answer, turn to page 89 for help with marking it.

6 Directed writing

You will be assessed on your ability to use either pre-released or unseen literary and non-literary extracts to write for **different purposes** and **different audiences**.

You may be asked, for example, to turn part of a play into a newspaper article; to continue writing in the same style as the original extract; to represent the material into a radio or television script. It is important that you are familiar with **a wide range of writing styles and conventions of particular genres**.

You will also be asked to write a **commentary** on the original piece of writing you have produced. In it you will be expected to consider the questions in terms of the original extract and the piece you have written.

Typical Exam Question

The text of the advertisement below appeared in the *Radio Times*.

Have you?

the value of experience

Well have you? You know, been there, done that?

Anyone who tells you the world's getting smaller hasn't driven a Suzuki lately. For over 30 years, Suzuki 4 × 4s have been expanding drivers' horizons, taking them as far as their imagination leads them. And sometimes beyond. For real adventures, you need a real 4 × 4. Like the new Suzuki Grand Vitara.

Underneath that smoothly-contoured bodyshell, the Grand Vitara is pure, uncompromising off-road engineering with a ladder-frame chassis that's strong enough and durable enough to take on the toughest of terrains. Long-travel suspension and high ground clearance let you ride easily over rocks, ruts and river-beds. The Drive Select 4 × 4 system, giving you all the traction and control you need – with an effortless switch to 2WD when you get back on the tarmac. You can choose from 2.0 litre petrol and Turbo Diesel engines or a gutsy 2.5 V6. Whatever Mother Nature's throwing at you outside, inside it's all comfort, space and relaxation. And wherever life takes you, the Grand Vitara offers unparalleled safety, comfort and driver satisfaction, all at a price that's a world away from other 4 × 4s. If you expect a lot from your car, we expect your call on 01892 707007

(a) In the style of the original extract, write the opening (around 120 words) of another advertisement promoting a household product for a similar audience.

(b) Compare the style and language of your advertisement with those of the original extract.

[Time allowed: 1 hour]

How to tackle this question

Before you begin writing you need to explore some specific points about the extract:

- Who is the **intended audience** for this passage? For instance, what kind of people read the *Radio Times*?

- What is the **purpose** of the writing? Is it to persuade, to inform or entertain?

- Can you recognise certain features of style and language that we associate with advertisements? For example, the use of informal questions, the way the text offers the reader a possible lifestyle (an aspirational approach); the way in which it offers the reader choices and possibilities; reassurance; the use of abstract nouns like 'comfort, space and relaxation'; the mixture of words that suggest luxury with those which imply strength and power; the insertion of technical jargon at various points.

- Don't try to produce something which is totally different in terms of content, style and language from the original – you could be making unnecessary difficulties for yourself!

You also need to decide which points your commentary should make:

- Do not waste time and space by spending too much time writing about the design and font style.

- You will gain higher marks by using **quotations** from both the original extract and your own piece and commenting on the **qualities** they bring to mind.

- Think about the way the advertisements address their readers **(the mode of address)** – see if it changes as they progress and the possible reasons why it may do so.

- Think about the specific **techniques** the advertisements use at different points: do they flatter the reader? Do they switch from a reassuring to a more hard-selling approach?

- Work through the passages in **short sections** looking for **similarities** and **differences** between sections in terms of **language** and **techniques**.

(a)

DO YOU?
LIKE TO CLEAN?

Well, do you? Anyone who says that cleaning's got easier probably has the Jupiter Atlas cleaner.

Jupiter have been at the front of the cleaning market for years with their sweeping, suction sensations. For real cleaning, you need a real cleaner. Beneath its beautifully shaped exterior beats a rugged and revolutionary motor. Strong enough to beat and clean the toughest of textures. You have all the controls at your fingertips. Switch from light to heavy clean with the precision-engineered feather-touch control panel...

(b)

In my piece of writing I tried to convey the sense of strength and precision suggested in the original. The car is seen as both delicate on the outside but very strong and impressive on the inside. I tried to show this in my piece by using phrases like 'Beneath its beautifully shaped exterior'. I noticed that there was alliteration in the car advertisement and I tried to include this in my advertisement too. There was also use of compound words and I used these in expressions such as 'precision-engineered' and 'feather-touch'...

John has successfully copied the appearance and the structural strength of the original piece.

John has tried to capture the personal mode of address at the start, as well as the use of short sentence structure and alliteration.

John has shown in his commentary that he is aware of features such as alliteration.

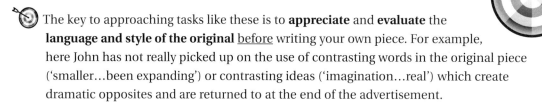

How to score higher marks

- The key to approaching tasks like these is to **appreciate** and **evaluate** the **language and style of the original** <u>before</u> writing your own piece. For example, here John has not really picked up on the use of contrasting words in the original piece ('smaller…been expanding') or contrasting ideas ('imagination…real') which create dramatic opposites and are returned to at the end of the advertisement.

- These could have been added to his own piece. Try to **list** the stylistic and linguistic features of the original before writing your own piece. By doing this you will also be clear what your commentary will contain before completing your own creative writing.

- John's commentary is good but would benefit from more **brief quotations** from the original extract and **comments on their effects** (for example, the contrast between the imaginary and real worlds). At times his commentary is in danger of identifying surface features such as alliteration without really suggesting their possible effects.

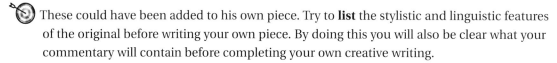

Typical Exam Question

The following is a complete ghost story.

She was standing by the river looking at the stepping-stones and remembering each one. There was the round unsteady stone, the pointed one, the flat one in the middle – the safe stone where you could stand and look round. The next wasn't so safe, for when the river was full the water flowed over it and even when it showed dry it was slippery. But after that it was easy and soon she was standing on the other side.

The road was much wider than it used to be but the work had been done carelessly. The felled trees had not been cleared away and the bushes looked trampled. Yet it was the same road and she walked along feeling extraordinarily happy.

It was a fine day, a blue day. The only thing was that the sky had a glassy look that she didn't remember. That was the only word she could think of. Glassy. She turned the corner, saw that what had been the old pavement had been taken up, and there too the road was much wider, but it had the same unfinished look.

She came to the worn stone steps that led up to the house and her heart began to beat. The screw pine was gone, so was the mock summer-house called the ajoupa, but the clove tree was still there and at the top of the steps the rough lawn stretched away, just as she remembered it. She stopped and looked towards the house that had been added to and painted white. It was strange to see a car standing in front of it.

There were two children under the big mango tree, a boy and a little girl, and she waved to them and called 'Hallo' but they didn't answer her or turn their heads. …

The grass was yellow in the hot sunlight as she walked towards them. When she was quite close she called again, shyly: 'Hallo.' Then, 'I used to live here once,' she said.

Still they didn't answer. When she said for the third time 'Hallo' she was quite near them. Her arms went out instinctively with the longing to touch them.

It was the boy who turned. His grey eyes looked straight into hers. His expression didn't change. He said: 'Hasn't it gone cold all of a sudden. D'you notice? Let's go in.' 'Yes let's,' said the girl.

Her arms fell to her sides as she watched them running across the grass to the house. That was the first time she knew.

(a) This story is typical of the writer's style and is to form part of her *Collected Ghost Stories* which are about to be published. You have been asked to write the blurb for the book cover encouraging people to buy the publication.

(b) Write a commentary on your piece of writing, comparing its linguistic and literary features to those of the original story.

[Time allowed: 1 hour]

How to tackle this question

You need to explore some specific points about the extract <u>before</u> you begin writing:

- Who is the **intended audience** for this story? Remember you need to promote the book in a positive way without overdoing it. You will therefore need to communicate some of the themes of the writing as well as some aspects of its language and style. For example, there is a clash between the seeming innocence of the narrator and the world in which she lives; the style is descriptive in terms of setting but distant too – we never know who these characters are.

- Before you begin writing, highlight some of the themes and language features of the original story so that you can itemise these and focus on them in the blurb. Decide the order they should go in.

- Think about the **style and language** we might expect to find in a typical blurb for certain kinds of fiction writing. For example, for ghost stories we might expect to find the use of adjectives that suggest suspense and intrigue, and terms which suggest that the author creates worlds we fear and which are beyond our normal experience. You might also include suggestions why this particular writer is different to other authors who write ghost stories. What distinguishes her work in particular?

You also need to decide which points your commentary should make:

- You should explain some of the **themes** and **ideas** you saw in the original story.

- You should use **quotations** from the original story and your own writing and comment on the **qualities** they convey.

- You should compare the different **approaches** and **purposes** of both pieces: the ghost story keeps the reader at a distance and uses adjectives which play on our senses, while the blurb should try to engage much more personally and use words which entice and intrigue us. In other words, the story does not spell things out while the blurb tries to be more explicit about themes and style.

(a) Mysterious yet simple; the ordinary giving way to the unexpected; polished description; the turn of phrase. These are just some of the thoughts that this new collection of stories provoke. From her early writing right through to her more recent return to the form, you will be led into dark worlds even though there is sunlight; a world where past and present merge; a world where some can see and some can't; a world where the familiar things are not quite what they seem; a world where the innocence of children can conceal the most discomforting experiences. Some of these stories are unusual in the way they play around with points of view, the order of events; other shock through their simplicity. Read them and be drawn into unknown areas — or ones you would rather avoid.

(b) In my piece of writing I have tried to refer to both the themes and style of the given story without giving too much away. What struck me most about the story was its sense of opposites — light and dark, living and dead, past and present.
The author uses the present tense to highlight how cut off the narrator is from the other children. It is also interesting the way that the author uses an apparent everyday situation of children playing to create an innocent feel to the story but also leaves the reader to work out the ending.

In terms of language the original story is very precise in its use of position and place. Everything is described exactly: 'There was the round unsteady stone, the pointed one, the flat one...' These details highlight the narrator's familiarity with the place and the depths of the memories. Yet it is the interruption of this precise style that indicates something is not right: 'The only thing was the sky had a glassy look that she didn't remember. That was the only word she could think of. Glassy.' The precise use of colours and textures all the way through the story also enhances the depth of the narrator's familiarity with the place... In my blurb I could not adapt this kind of style. I had to try and capture the feelings of the piece by using adjectives such as 'mysterious' and 'polished'; I had to indicate the nature of the content through implication without giving away details, to persuade the reader that the stories may appeal to their 'darker' thoughts...

Why this answer scores high marks

Linda has captured both the **content** and **stylistic** aspects of the original story in her blurb. She has addressed the idea of an apparently simple world hiding darker possibilities; the feeling of innocence lost in a separate location; the unusual sense of the first person narrator and the way the reader is left to work out the events of the situation.

She has drawn the reader into a sense of the **range of material** the author has produced over time.

She has captured some aspects of the story's style (such as the lightness concealing darker worlds) without getting bogged down in specific details.

Her commentary addresses aspects of **style** through apt use of **quotation** and she is aware of the **progression** of the story and style, seeing how the precision is interrupted. She refers to the use of **colour** and **textures** and the possible reasons why they are used.

Her approach shows the ability to **compare** fictional writing with the non-fictional writing of a blurb and the different **purposes** of both.

Most importantly, Linda **listed** the **stylistic** and **linguistic** features of the original before writing the blurb and so prepared the main ingredients of her commentary at the same time. **Remember to do the same.**

She has also demonstrated the ability to use **quotations** and to **comment** on them.

Don't forget ...

Decide on the intended **audience** and the **purpose** of the piece of writing <u>before</u> you begin.

Think about the **style** and **typical language features** and **conventions** of the piece you have been asked to write.

Plan ahead and **list** the features you are going to include in your creative writing.

Remember to use **quotations** in your commentary from both the original extract and your own writing. Comment on their **effects**.

In your commentary work through the passages in **short sections** looking for **similarities** and **differences** between each section.

The passage below describes the writer's experience of travelling on the subway in New York.

When people say the subway frightens them, they are not being silly or irrational. It is no good saying how cheap or how fast it is. The subway is frightening. It is also very easy to get lost in the subway, and the person who is lost in New York City has a serious problem. New Yorkers make it their business to avoid getting lost.

It is the stranger who gets lost. It is the stranger who follows people hurrying into the stairwell: subway entrances are just dark holes in the sidewalk – the stations are below ground. There is nearly always a bus-stop near the subway entrance. People waiting at a bus-stop have a special pitying gaze for people entering the subway. It is sometimes not pity, but fear; bewilderment, curiosity; or fatalism; often they look like miners'wives watching their menfolk going down the pit.

The stranger's sense of disorientation down below is immediate. The station is all tile and iron and dampness; it has bars and turnstiles and steel grates. It has the look of an old prison or a monkey cage.

Buying a token, the stranger may ask directions, but the token booth – reinforced, burglar-proof, bullet-proof – renders the reply incoherent. And subway directions are a special language: 'A train… Downtown… Express to the Shuttle… Change at Ninety-sixth for the two… Uptown… The Lex… CC… LL… The Local….'

Most New Yorkers refer to the subway by the now-obsolete forms 'IND', 'IRT', 'BMT'. No one intentionally tries to confuse the stranger; it is just that, where the subway is concerned, precise directions are very hard to convey.

Verbal directions are incomprehensible, written ones are defaced. The signboards and subway maps are indiscernible beneath layers of graffiti...

(a) Basing your answer on the extract, write the opening to a script for a promotional film sponsored by the owners of the New York subway which tries to persuade visitors to the city to use the facility.

(b) Write a commentary which compares the style and language of your piece to the original extract.

[Time allowed: 1 hour]

After writing your answer, turn to page 91 for help with marking it.

This chapter contains a range of exam questions for you to try answering. They cover all the types of questions you have already met in earlier chapters in this book.

Once you have written your answers, turn to pages 92–96 for help with grading them.

Prose fiction and non-fiction

There may be occasions where you will be asked to compare fiction and non-fiction texts during your AS course.

Each of the passages below describes an attempted escape from prison. In Passage A the writer explains how she escaped with some help while Passage B is taken from a novel and describes the failure of a spy and his accomplice to escape.

Passage A

I wore a leather jacket, to protect me from branches in the woods, so I got through the woods without a scratch. I'd never been in those woods before, and it was scary. Woods at night are always creepy, and when you're in a hurry, even more so. I didn't want to lose an eye to a low-hanging branch; nor did I want to fall into a hidden ravine and break a leg. I didn't know whether there were any ravines. The woods sloped generally uphill from the housing unit to the highway beyond. I was still within the perimeter of the fence.

It was hot, and very dark in the woods. I sweated profusely; I had the hood of my sweatshirt over my head. My heart was pounding. I was afraid I would hyperventilate because I was panting like a horse. The air seemed thick and rank. I just wanted to get through those woods!

I went up, and farther up, and eventually I could see light at the end of the woods, I was running toward the light, scrambling over fallen trees, crossing one small ravine on a deadfall bridge, like a balance beam, but I just went, driving myself, trying not to panic, trying to keep going.

I reached the fence. It was tall, maybe nine or ten feet, with barbed wire at the top. I wrapped my belt around the barbed wire and I pulled it taut, and no sooner had I done so than I heard a car coming.

I didn't know if it was Nick, but I couldn't risk being seen at the top of the fence,

so I jumped down, ran for cover and waited. It could be a prison van doing a perimeter check.

When the truck had passed, I tried again.

This time I became hooked on the barbed wire. It snagged my pants, and I felt it tear into my leg. I yanked at it, and the barbs raked my leg, but I freed myself.

I left half my pant leg on the wire. Talk about fibre evidence!

Later, I saw three or four big gashes in my leg. It looked as though I'd been attacked by a mountain lion - four big claw marks in the flesh. I worried about infection, but it healed eventually.

I was out!

I had to run for cover.

The truck that had passed hadn't been Nick after all. We two amateurs had got the timing down pat. Nick showed up right on time.

A witness at his trial later swore he'd seen Nick parked near the fence where he picked me up. It still amazes me what lies people will tell, just to get into the papers or on television. Nick never parked anywhere - we had worked that out ahead of time. Drive up and down twenty times if you must, I'd warned him, but don't ever stop, it will only attract attention. He'd agreed, and did as I suggested.

He pulled up, I jumped in, and we sped off. To freedom!

I'd made it! It was an amazing feeling. My heart was still going. My adrenaline levels must have been off the charts! Ecstasy mingled with fear.

I scrunched down and started peeling layers of clothes off to cool myself. I took my leather jacket off, then my sweatshirt, down to a tank top. Hand in hand, with Guns 'n' Roses blasting on the tape player, we just drove straight through to Canada. It took us all night.

It was mid-morning by the time we got to Canada. There were some things in our favor. I was in good shape and I was suntanned, so I didn't look like the stereotypical jailbird. We were sitting there holding hands like an ordinary couple.

'What's your business in Canada?' the border officer asked.

Could I have told them an earful! Refuge, I wanted to say.

'We're on honeymoon,' I said.

'Okay then, have a nice time,' she said, smiling and waving us oft.

Freedom! I rolled down the window and let the breeze speed through my hair.

The sun beat furiously over the tops of the pine trees. The sky was a brilliant blue.

I looked over at Nick and said, 'Well, maybe there is a God.' Me, an unwavering atheist for so many years!

Passage B

They walked quickly, Leamas glancing over his shoulder from time to time to make sure she was following. As he reached the end of the alley, he stopped, drew into the shadow of a doorway and looked at his watch.

'Two minutes,' he whispered.

She said nothing. She was staring straight ahead towards the wall, and the black ruins rising behind it.

'Two minutes,' Leamas repeated.

Before them was a strip of thirty yards. It followed the wall in both directions. Perhaps seventy yards to their right was a watch tower; the beam of its searchlight played along the strip. The thin rain hung in the air, so that the light from the arclamps was sallow and chalky, screening the world beyond. There was no one to be seen; not a sound. An empty stage.

The watch tower's searchlight began feeling its way along the wall towards them, hesitant; each time it rested they could see the separate bricks and the careless lines of mortar hastily put on. As they watched the beam stopped immediately in front of them. Leamas looked at his watch.

'Ready?' he asked.

She nodded.

Taking her arm he began walking deliberately across the strip. Liz wanted to run, but he held her so tightly that she could not. They were half-way towards the wall now, the brilliant semicircle of light drawing them forward, the beam directly above them. Leamas was determined to keep Liz very close to him, as if he were afraid that Mundt would not keep his word and somehow snatch her away at the last moment.

They were almost at the wall when the beam darted to the North leaving them momentarily in total darkness. Still holding Liz's arm, Leamas guided her forward blindly, his left hand reaching ahead of him until suddenly he felt the coarse, sharp contact of the cinder brick. Now he could discern the wall and, looking upwards, the triple strand of wire and the cruel hooks which held it. Metal wedges, like climbers' pitons, had been driven into the brick. Seizing the highest one, Leamas pulled himself quickly upwards until he had reached the top of the wall. He tugged sharply at the lower strand of wire and it came towards him, already cut.

'Come on,' he whispered urgently, 'start climbing.'

Laying himself flat he reached down, grasped her upstretched hand and began drawing her slowly upwards as her foot found the first metal rung.

Suddenly the whole world seemed to break into flame; from everywhere, from above and beside them, massive lights converged, bursting upon them with savage accuracy.

Leamas was blinded, he turned his head away, wrenching wildly at Liz's arm. Now she was swinging free; he thought she had slipped and he called frantically, still drawing her upwards. He could see nothing – only a mad confusion of colour dancing in his eyes.

Then came the hysterical wail of sirens, orders frantically shouted. Half kneeling astride the wall he grasped both her arms in his, and began dragging her to him inch by inch, himself on the verge of falling.

Compare the two extracts. In your answer you should:
• consider the use of vocabulary and expression;
• the means by which both writers try to create dramatic tension.

[Time allowed: 1 hour]

How to tackle this question

- Divide each passage into **sections** so that you can look for any **similarities** and **differences** between them.

- Look at the **use of voice** in each passage. What is the effect of using **first person** in Passage A and the **authorial voice** in Passage B?

- Compare the use of **setting** and **descriptive terms** in both passages. How do they contribute towards the **dramatic tension**?

- Compare the **vocabulary** and **expression** in both extracts.

- Consider the **use of syntax** in both extracts. What differences can you notice and what are their effects?

Q1

The first poem below was written by Rupert Brooke during the First World War. The second poem was written by Keith Douglas during the Second World War. The title is German for 'forget-me-not' and the poem describes how he came across an enemy soldier during the fighting in the deserts of North Africa.

Poem A

If I should die. think only this of me:
That there's some corner of a foreign field
That is for ever England. There shall be
In that rich earth a richer dust concealed:
A dust whom England bore, shaped, made aware,
Gave, once, her flowers to love, her ways to roam.
A body of England's, breathing English air,
Washed by the rivers, blest by suns of home.

And think, this heart, all evil shed away,
A pulse in the eternal mind, no less
Gives somewhere back the thoughts by England given;
Her sights and sounds; dreams happy as her day;
And laughter, learnt of friends: and gentleness.
In hearts at peace, under an English heaven.

Poem B

VERGISSMEINNICHT

Three weeks gone and the combatants gone
returning over the nightmare ground
we found the place again, and found
the soldier sprawling in the sun.

The frowning barrel of his gun
overshadowing. As we came on
that day, he hit my tank with one
like the entry of a demon.

Look. Here in the gunpit spoil
the dishonoured picture of his girl
who has put: *Steffi. Vergissmeinnicht*
in a copybook gothic script.

We see him almost with content,
abased, and seeming to have paid
and mocked at by his own equipment
that's hard and good when he's decayed.

But she would weep to see today
how on his skin the swart flies move;
the dust upon the paper eye
and the burst stomach like a cave.

For here the lover and killer are mingled
who had one body and one heart.
And death who had the soldier singled
has done the lover mortal hurt.

Write a critical appreciation of both poems. In your answer you should:
• compare their use of description and tone;
• comment on their use of form and language.

[Time allowed: 1 hour]

How to tackle this question

- Remember to divide each poem into **sections** so you can look for any **similarities** and **differences** between them.

- Consider the rather gentle and thoughtful **tone** of Poem A with the rather harsh opening of Poem B. Do the **tone** and **description** change in Poem B? What images of war are conveyed by the poems' different tones?

- Look at the **use of imagery** in Poem A and its use of **syntax** and the rather brutal **imagery** of Poem B.

- Comment on the use of **rhyme, word length** and **sound** in Poem B. Remember to comment on the **sonnet form** of Poem A. Compare it to the **form** of Poem B.

The poem below was written by Carol Ann Duffy.

Recognition

Things get away from one.
I've let myself go, I know.
Children? I've had three
and don't even know them.

I strain to remember a time
when my body felt lighter.
Years. My face is swollen
with regrets. I put powder on,

but it flakes off. I love him,
through habit, but the proof
has evaporated. He gets upset.
I tried to do all the essentials

on one trip. Foolish, yes,
but I was weepy all morning.
Quiche. A blond boy swung me up
in his arms and promised the earth.

You see, this came back to me
as I stood on the scales.
I wept. Shallots. In the window,
creamy ladies held a pose

which left me clogged and old.
The waste. I'd forgotten my purse,
fumbled; the shopgirl gaped at me,
compassionless. Claret. I blushed.

Cheese. Kleenex. *It did happen.*
I lay in my slip on wet grass,
laughing. Years. I had to rush out,
blind in a hot flush, and bumped

into an anxious, dowdy matron
who touched the cold mirror
and stared at me. Stared
and said I'm sorry sorry sorry.

Write a critical appreciation of the poem. In your answer you should:
• comment on the tone of the poem;
• consider the use of vocabulary.

[Time allowed: 1 hour]

How to tackle this question

● Remember to divide the poem into **sections** so you can look for **similarities** and **differences** between them.

● Look at the **use of voice** in the poem. Is this a reliable narrator?

● Consider the way it **contrasts** present and past narratives.

● Examine the way these narratives help to create the **tone** of the poem.

● Comment on the use of **syntax** and **phrasing**.

Speech and dialogue

Q1

The passage below is taken from a televised speech given by the American President Richard Nixon in April 1973.

Nixon is responding to an investigation into Watergate. Watergate was the term used by the media to describe a sequence of events in which employees from Nixon's own political party had burgled the headquarters of his main political opponents. Nixon had authorised the burglary himself (a serious offence for a President) but he skirts carefully around this issue in his speech.

Whatever may have appeared to have been the case before – whatever improper activities may yet be discovered in connexion with this whole sordid affair – I want the American people, I want you, to know beyond the shadow of a doubt that during my term as President, justice will be pursued fairly, fully, and impartially, no matter who is involved. This office is a sacred trust and I am determined to be worthy of that trust.

Who, then, is to blame for what happened in this case?

For specific criminal actions by specific individuals, those who committed those actions must, of course, bear the liability and pay the penalty. For the fact that alleged improper actions took place within the White House or within my campaign organization, the easiest course would be for me to blame those to whom I delegated the responsibility to run the campaign. But that would be a cowardly thing to do. I will not place the blame on subordinates, on people whose zeal exceeded their judgement, and who may have done wrong in a cause they deeply believed to be right. In any organization, the man at the top must bear the responsibility. That responsibility, therefore, belongs here, in this office. I accept it. And I pledge to you tonight, from this office, that I will do everything in my power to ensure that the guilty are brought to justice, and that such abuses are purged from our political processes in the years to come, long after I have left this office.

When I think of this office – of what it means – I think of all the things that I want to accomplish for this nation – of all the things I want to accomplish for you.

On Christmas Eve, during my terrible personal ordeal of the renewed bombing of North Vietnam, which after twelve years of war, finally helped to bring America peace with honor, I wrote out some of the goals for my second term as President. Let me read them to you.

'To make it possible for our children, and for our children's children, to live in a world of peace.

'To make this country be more than ever a land of opportunity – of equal opportunity, full opportunity for every American.

'To provide jobs for all who can work, and generous help for all who cannot.

'To establish a climate of decency, and civility, in which each person respects the feelings and dignity and the God-given rights of his neighbor.

'To make this a land in which each person can dare to dream, can live his dreams - not in fear, but in hope – proud of his community, proud of his country, proud of what America has meant to himself and the world.'

These are great goals. I believe we can, we must work for them. We can achieve them. But we cannot achieve these goals unless we dedicate ourselves to another goal.

We must maintain the integrity of the White House, and that integrity must be real, not transparent. There can be no white-wash in the White House.

We must reform our political process ridding it not only of violations of the law, but also of the ugly mob violence, and other inexcusable campaign tactics that have been too often practised and too readily accepted by one side to the excesses or expected excesses of the other side. Two wrongs do not make a right.

I looked at my own calendar this morning up at Camp David as I was working on this speech. It showed exactly 1,361 days remaining in my term. I want these to be the best days in America's history, because I love America. I deeply believe that America is the hope of the world, and I know that in the quality and wisdom of the leadership America gives lies the only hope for millions of people all over the world, that they can live their lives in peace and freedom. We must be worthy of that hope, in every sense of the word.

Tonight, I ask for your prayers to help me in everything that I do through the days of my Presidency to be worthy of their hopes and of yours. God bless America and God bless each and every one of you.

- Comment on the speaker's style and use of language in the passage.
- In the style of the passage, write a speech (around 100 words) in which a well-known figure of your choice, contemporary or historical, denies any wrong doing.

[Time allowed: 1 hour]

How to tackle this question

- Remember that this is not a transcript of natural spontaneous speech. It has been written down and crafted to achieve certain effects and is there to persuade the listeners.

- **Highlight key words and phrases** and to divide the passage into **smaller sections** so you can look for **similarities** and **differences** between them.

- Assess the **audience** for the speech, its **context** and its **purpose**.

- Look at the **mode of address** and **register**.

- Consider the **rhetorical devices** the speaker uses.

The extract below contains a fictional presentation of a criminal speaking. It is taken from *Great Expectations* by Charles Dickens.

He gave me a most tremendous dip and roll, so that the church jumped over its own weather-cock. Then, he held me by the arms in an upright position on the top of the stone, and went on in these fearful terms:

'You bring me, to-morrow morning early, that file and them wittles[1]. You bring the lot to me, at that old Battery over yonder. You do it, and you never dare to say a word or dare to make a sign concerning your having seen such a person as me, or any person sumever, and you shall be let to live. You fail, or you go from my words in any partickler, no matter how small it is, and your heart and your liver shall be tore out, roasted and ate. Now, I ain't alone, as you may think I am. There's a young man hid with me, in comparison with which young man I am a Angel. That young man hears the words I speak. That young man has a secret way pecooliar to himself, of getting at a boy, and at his heart, and at his liver. It is in wain for a boy to attempt to hide himself from that young man. A boy may lock his door, may be warm in bed, may tuck himself up, may draw the clothes over his head, may think himself comfortable and safe, but that young man will softly creep and creep his way to him and tear him open. I am a keeping that young man from harming of you at the present moment, with great difficulty. I find it wery hard to hold that young man off of your inside. Now, what do you say?'

I said that I would get him the file, and I would get him what broken bits of food I could, and I would come to him at the Battery, early in the morning.

¹ wittles – food and drink

Write a critical appreciation of the passage. In your answer you should:
• consider the expression and vocabulary;
• consider how these contribute to the characterisation in the passage.

[Time allowed: 1 hour]

How to tackle this question

- When studying fictional dialogue, try to discover how the writer has conveyed the ideas of **dialect** and **accent**. Has **phonetic spelling** been used? Are there certain **words or phrases** that indicate the speaker comes from a particular place or region?

- In the same way, **compare how different characters speak** in the passage. Do they all talk in the same way? Do some have a regional dialect and vocabulary? Do some speak in **received pronunciation** (the idea of a form of Standard English which essentially lacks an accent and follows 'correct' rules of pronunciation, grammar and expression).

- If there are **contrasts**, what kinds of **attitudes and values** are suggested by the characters? Do some of the talkers seem more or less educated, more authoritative, to have more prestige?

Drama

Q1

The extract below is taken from *Macbeth* by William Shakespeare. It shows the reactions of Macbeth and Lady Macbeth just after they have murdered King Duncan in their castle. Macbeth hopes that killing Duncan will allow him to become king.

Enter Macbeth

Macb.   I have done the deed – Didst thou not hear a noise?

Lady M.	I heard the owl scream and the crickets cry.
	Did you not speak?
Macb.	When?
Lady M.	Now.
Macb.	As I descended?
Lady M.	Ay.
Macb.	Hark!
	Who lies i' th'second chamber?
Lady M.	Donalbain.
Macb.	This is a sorry sight.
Lady M.	A foolish thought to say a sorry sight.
Macb.	There's one did laugh in's sleep, and one cried,
	'Murther!'
	That they did wake each other: I stood and heard them;
	But they did say their prayers, and address'd them
	Again to sleep.
Lady M.	There are two lodg'd together.
Macb.	One cried, 'God bless us!' and 'Amen,' the other,
	As they had seen me with these hangman's hands.
	List'ning their fear, I could not say, 'Amen,'
	When they did say, 'God bless us.'
Lady M.	Consider it not so deeply.
Macb.	But wherefore could not I pronounce 'Amen'?
	I had most need of blessing, and 'Amen' stuck in my throat.
Lady M.	These deeds must not be thought
	As I descended?
Macb.	
Lady M.	After these ways: so, it will make us mad.
Macb.	Methought, I heard a voice cry, 'Sleep no more!
	Macbeth doth murther sleep,' - the innocent sleep;
	Sleep, that knits up the ravell'd sleave of care,
	The death of each day's life, sore labour's bath,
	Balm of hurt minds, great Nature's second course,
	Chief nourisher in life's feast;
Lady M.	What do you mean?
Macb.	Still it cried, 'Sleep no more!' to all the house:
	'Glamis hath murther'd sleep, and therefore Cawdor
	Can sleep no more, Macbeth shall sleep no more!

Lady M.	Who was it that thus cried? Why, worthy Thane,
	You do unbend your noble strength, to think
	So brainsickly of things. Go, get some water,
	And wash this filthy witness from your hand. -
	Why did you bring these daggers from the place?
	They must lie there: go, carry them, and smear
	The sleepy grooms with blood.
Macb.	I'll go no more:
	I am afraid to think what I have done; Look on't again I dare not.
Lady M.	Infirm of purpose!
	Give me the daggers. The sleeping, and the dead,
	Are but as pictures; 'tis the eye of childhood
	That fears a painted devil. If he do bleed,
	I'll gild the faces of the grooms withal,
	For it must seem their guilt. *[Exit. Knocking within]*
Macb.	'Whence is that knocking? -
	How is't with me, when every noise appals me?
	What hands are here? Ha! they pluck out mine eyes.
	Will all great Neptune's ocean wash this blood
	Clean from my hand? No, this my hand will rather
	The multitudinous seas incarnadine,
	Making the green one red.
	[Re-enter Lady Macbeth]
Lady M.	My hands are of your colour; but I shame
	To wear a heart so white. *[Knock.]* I hear a knocking
	At the south entry: – retire we to our chamber.
	A little water clears us of this deed:
	How easy is it then! Your constancy
	Hath left you unattended. – *[Knock.]* Hark! more knocking.
	Get on your night-gown, lest occasion call us,
	And show us to be watchers. – Be not lost
	So poorly in your thoughts.
Macb.	To know my deed, 'twere best not know myself.

Consider the presentation of the characters of Macbeth and Lady Macbeth here. In your answer you should:
• assess how the dramatic situation shapes their behaviour;
• comment on each character's use of language.

[Time allowed: 1 hour]

- Divide the passage into **sections** so that you can look for **similarities** and **differences** between them.

- Consider who is in **control** here and the way that the characterisation seems to work by **contrast**.

- Look at how each character seems to **develop** as the scene progresses. What differences can you sense?

- Comment on the **vocabulary** and **imagery** that each character uses.

- Consider the way that they **speak to each other** and how Macbeth seems to speak to himself.

The following extract comes from the play *The Typists* (1963) by Murray Schisgal.

[SYLVIA PAYTON enters from right. She is late for work. She throws her coat on the hanger, rushes across the room, deposits her lunch bag in the top drawer of a cabinet, removes cover from her typewriter and begins typing rapidly, glancing anxiously at the employer's door. In a moment she relaxes; she types slowly and hums to herself; she takes her comb and mirror from her pocketbook and fixes her hair. The front door opens. She puts everything away and without turning to see who has entered she starts to type rapidly again. PAUL CUNNINGHAM approaches, passing his lunch bag from hand to hand.]

Paul	Good morning. I'm Paul Cunningham. I was hired yesterday by... *[Laughing uneasily]* That's funny. I forgot his name. You'll have to excuse me. First day on the job ... I'm a little nervous. It was the boss who hired me, though; at least that's what he said.
Sylvia	I know. He told me. *[Rising, shaking his hand]* Sylvia. Miss Sylvia Payton. Glad to meet you, Mr Cunningham. If you'll hang up your coat I'll show you what you have to do.
Paul	I'm sorry I'm late, Miss Payton. I got on the wrong train by mistake. Generally you'll find that I'm a pretty prompt person.
Sylvia	Oh, that's all right. Just make sure it doesn't happen too often. He's very strict when it comes to being here on time. And now that he's made me responsible for this whole department.... Of course I won't say anything to him about this morning.
Paul	I'd appreciate that a lot.
Sylvia	Don't even mention it. Believe me, I didn't ask him to be made a supervisor. I don't like telling anyone what to do; that's part of my nature, I guess. You give me your lunch bag, Mr Cunningham. I'll put it in the file cabinet; that's where I keep mine.
Paul	Thanks. I was sure lucky to get this job. I go to school at night and a lot of firms don't hire you if they know that.
Sylvia	You must be a very ambitious person. What are you studying?
Paul *[proudly]*.	Law. Another three years and I should get my degree. Boy, that's one day I'm looking forward to.

Sylvia	It must be extremely difficult to have a job and go to school at the same time.
Paul	It's been real rough so far. But it has its advantages. When I get out, I'm going to have the satisfaction of knowing I did it myself, with my own sweat and my own money; that's more than most fellows my age can say.
Sylvia	How true that is.
Paul	Listen, I have an uncle who's a lawyer, a pretty darn famous lawyer, too. Francis T. Cunningham. You ask anybody in the legal field about Francis T. Cunningham and they'll tell you how much he's worth. Well, if I wanted to, I just have to pick up that phone, give him a ring and my worrying days would be over. But that's not for me; no, sir. I'll do it alone or I'm not doing it at all.

Sylvia *[uncovers PAUL'S typewriter, opens directory for him].*

> I think you're a hundred per cent right. You know, I once went with a boy – it was nothing serious, it could have been, but ... I won't go into that now. Anyway, his father was helping him through medical school. He didn't have to earn a penny of his own. Do you think he finished? What happened was that his father remarried and stopped giving him money. He fell completely apart; you never saw anything like it.

Paul	There's no substitute for character.

Write a commentary on the extract. In your answer you should:

• consider the relationship between the characters;

• comment on their use of vocabulary and expression.

[Time allowed: 1 hour]

How to tackle this question

● Divide the passage into **sections** so that you can look for any **similarities** and **differences** between them.

● Consider who seems to be in **control** here.

● Comment on the use of **stage directions**. What do they add to our understanding of the **situation** and the **characters**?

● Explore the ways in which the characters **speak to each other**. Is any character **putting on an act**?

● Do the characters seem to **develop** or **change** as the scene unfolds?

● Study the characters' use of **vocabulary** and **expression**. Is there much **imagery** here or not? What is the **effect** of this?

Q1

The advertisement below encourages readers to reconsider their views about the attractiveness, style and efficiency of heating products.

Things are
HOTTING up
on the design front

A revolution in home heating has taken place – and it's causing quite a stir!
Who thinks about radiators? Practically no one. But if you did, you'd probably think oblong, white, functional ... and that's about it.

Until now. Because the whole concept of home heating has just been turned on its head. In fact, with the help of some of the UK's and Europe's leading contemporary designers and manufacturers, British Gas has created what can only be described as a radiator revolution.

CENTRAL HEATING WILL NEVER BE THE SAME AGAIN.
Where once you had oblong, you can now have tall curves of gleaming chrome, or minimalist ultra-fine heating tubes. Where once you could choose any colour as long as it was white, now you have a positive palette, including red, green and gold. Inspiring, exciting and definitely different, this new generation of radiators gives you the scope to totally transform any room in your home.

Boilers too have had a makeover. Today's high-efficiency and condenser boilers are all smaller, slimmer and more discreet – so you can tuck them away unseen. They're more economical and affordable than ever before, and their increased efficiency means you could save up to 20% on your gas bills.

CENTRAL HEATING SYSTEM BY DESIGN.
Should all this choice make it difficult for you to decide which heating system is the one for you ... well, British Gas has thought of that too. An expert Technical Adviser can visit your home and design the perfect system with you. Then all the installation work is carried out with the minimum of fuss by highly trained engineers.

Though it seems a little premature to start thinking about central heating now, it's actually a shrewd move. The British Gas summer sale is on until 31st August, so if you act now you could end up saving a considerable amount on your new system. It also makes sense to ensure your home's winter-proof before the cold weather arrives.

(a) As the writer of the piece you have been asked to produce a further advertisement promoting another household product. In the style of the original extract, write the advertisement (around 150 words).

(b) Compare your advertisement with the original one. In your answer you should focus on distinctive features of language such as register and vocabulary.

[Time allowed: 1 hour]

- Consider the intended **audience** of the advertisement.

- Divide the extract into **sections** so that you can look for **similarities** and **differences** between them.

- Before you write your own piece **highlight** the **key features** and **aspects of style** of the original so that you can **plan** your advertisement.

- Look at the **mode of address** and the **register** of the original advertisement.

- Does the advertisement offer an **aspirational** approach? Does it use **questions** or **abstract** nouns? Does it use **adjectives** or **imagery**?

- Look at the **syntax** and **vocabulary**. Are there any particular features?

The extracts below are taken from an advertisement which encourages people to use the cross-channel ferry to sample life in France.

With Brittany Ferries the time you spend on board is as much a part of a French holiday as buying a freshly-baked baguette. Your trip to France begins the moment you step aboard the ship and, while the cars may be travelling by ferry, the passengers are most surely on a cruise, relaxing in the comfortable lounges, the spacious bar, the stylish restaurant, with its superb French cuisine, enjoying the distractions on offer of live entertainment, video, cinemas, duty-free shops, boutiques, and above all, soaking up that unmistakable Gallic ambience.

'Spoilt for choice' is an expression which springs to mind as you consider where to go when you leave the quayside at Caen. Here you are on the threshold of Normandy's most beautiful scenery, like the valley of the Auge, Swiss Normandy, Deauville and Honfleur, with the choice of Brittany Ferries' selection of French gites, British holiday homes, chambres d'hotes or selected hotels in which to stay. And with the special six-day-return fare for a car and driver from only £62, a week spent basking in the pleasures of rural Normandy becomes something of a bargain.

Surprisingly it's only just over 250 miles from England, using the Britanny Ferries route from Portsmouth to Caen, to the picturesque medieval harbour of La Rochelle and places like the beautiful Ile de Ré, the peaceful meandering Charente and the fascinating Marais Poitevin, a green maze of tree-lined canals and rivers. If you've time, do stop for a while en-route to the Touraine, where magnificent chateaux like Chambord, Chinon, Chenonceaux and Blois wait to be explored.

It's an easy drive from Caen to Aquitaine, with the fabled vineyards of the Medoc and St Emilion, the great forest of the Landes and the glorious Atlantic beaches of Arcachon and Biarritz. A short drive to the east leads you into the beautiful countryside of the Dordogne and to some of France's prettiest villages.

St Malo has a charm which will tempt you to stay, and nearby are some of Brittany's finest beaches, but it's also the perfect start to a holiday in the western Loire, a comfortable drive away. There are magnificent chateaux, such as Angers and Saumur, the mysterious Pays de Retz, the pretty seaport of Pornic, the fine old resort of La Baule and, further south, the Vendée with the splendid beaches of St Jean-de-Monts and Les Sables d'Olonne.

You can discover the French land's end of Finistere, which is just an hour or so's motoring from the port of Roscoff using the Brittany Ferries route from Plymouth. Here too is Morbihan, steeped in folklore, where you will discover places such as the intriguing reed-fringed marshes of the Grande Briere and villages like Ile de Fedrun and the grey-stone village of Rochefort-en-Terre.

Santander is the gateway to Asturias, Cantabria and Galicia where magnificent sandy beaches are within an easy drive of the spectacular mountain scenery of the Picos de Europa, medieval villages like Santillana del Mar, the fjord-like rias of Galicia, the historic pilgrim city of Santiago de Compostela, and the secret countryside of northern Portugal.

Where to stay? Choice may be a problem here too; Brittany Ferries can offer 1000 self-catering British holiday homes throughout France from where you can buy mouthwatering produce in local markets and discover the delights of the local charcuterie and patisserie to take back and enjoy at your leisure. Or there are more than a thousand French gites to choose from, ranging from watermills to Breton cottages, poolside villas and lakeside retreats.

Alternatively, if touring is more to your taste, then the freedom of selected hotels and chambres d'hotes is the answer, either pre-booked or with vouchers for complete freedom of choice.

Throughout France and Spain, Brittany Ferries now offer more than 3000 carefully vetted properties and, with inclusive prices from as little as £252 for a week's self-catering for a family, the sheer pleasure of travelling the quiet scenic roads of France and Spain has never been more affordable.

(a) As the writer of the advertisement you have been asked to compose another one promoting another place of interest, either in Britain or abroad. In the style of the extract above, write the advertisement (around 200 words).

(b) Compare the style of your advertisement with the original one.

[Time allowed: 1 hour]

How to tackle this question

- Consider the intended **audience** of the advertisement.

- Divide the extract into **sections** so that you can look for **similarities** and **differences** between them.

- Before you write your own piece **highlight** the **key features** and **aspects of style** of the original so that you can **plan** your advertisement.

- Look at the **mode of address** and the **register** of the original advertisement.

- Look at the **use of adjectives** and **descriptive** terms.

- Consider the **use of French terms** in the advertisement.

Answers to Questions to try

Extracts from a Grade A answer

The first speaker, Mr Rochester, speaks in a very assertive way, almost seeming to declare his passion to an audience. He addresses Jane in a very formal way, using poetic and perhaps rather unreal language such as 'delicate and aerial'; he repeats the abstract noun 'beauty' three times at the beginning, almost idealising the woman he loves; although she is present, Rochester describes Jane as if she is someone else, a creature over which he has control and possession: 'I will attire my Jane in satin and lace…'. She is a creature he wishes to shape and mould into a romantic symbol. His vocabulary implies she is some sort of mythical and poetic creation, with 'roses in her hair' and 'a priceless veil'. For a while he lapses into more recognisable and familiar language but even here he is the one issuing orders and taking control: 'I told you we will be married in four weeks. The wedding is to take place quietly…' He returns to his idealisation and poetic and archaic language; the stilted nature of his dialogue conveys the unreal and strange mood he is creating, ignoring the protests of the figure actually in front of him. he draws on terms like 'waft' and 'sojourn'; he carries on comparing her to some mythical figure such as a 'sylph'. Indeed this idealisation is almost religious; she is an 'angel'; the repeated use of such words and phrase suggests the rather fantastical ideas he has; she seems to be there for his needs rather than her own because he will revisit his old haunts from ten years ago as a refreshed and restored man, showing off his partner as a trophy.

In contrast, Jane's words seem to be full of mild protest and self-deprecation. She tries to counter his words by using opposite adjectives to those he employs: 'Puny and insignificant, you mean'. Unlike Rochester, she is trying to speak directly to the listener and is not imagining romantic ideals. She directs her comments to him all the time, trying to pull him back: 'You are dreaming… you are sneering', 'Shall I travel – and with you'. She is unsure of his tone at the start but gradually grows in confidence and asserts her opinions. By the close she is laughing at his ideas and 'asserted' her opinions strongly. She has gradually moved from being unsure to being down to earth and realistic: 'Don't flatter me… I am not an angel… .I will be myself'. She is trying to impose her own identity on a man who seems to think of her as some other figure, to remind him that she exists in the here and now not in his imagination or the future. For most of the passage she has addressed from a position of inferiority, seeming still an employee rather than an equal partner. She refers to him as 'sir' until her final piece of dialogue where she speaks to him with a degree of authority. The use of her narrative voice allows to see the distance between them as she offers her opinions of Rochester: 'I felt he was either deluding himself, or trying to delude me'…

How to grade your answer

Grade A

You have sensed the use of **contrast** between the characters, especially in the use of **vocabulary** and **dialogue** and have shown these differences through the use of **brief quotations**.

You have sensed the **mood** of the passage. You have sensed that Rochester speaks in a rather romantic and far-fetched manner in **comparison** to Jane who is much more realistic and down to earth.

You have **identified** and **commented** on **what** the characters say and **how** they say it. For example, you have noticed how Rochester speaks about Jane in a rather poetic and stilted manner and issues commands, almost ignoring her presence. You have seen that Jane grows in confidence, trying to pull him back to the present and gradually losing her sense of inferiority in the way she addresses Rochester as 'sir'.

Grade C

You have sensed some of the use of contrast in the vocabulary and dialogue but have not used enough brief quotations to develop your insights.

You have approached some aspects of the **mood** of the passage but need to **develop** more comparisons between Rochester and Jane's attitudes.

You have identified some of **what** the characters say but have **not fully developed** comments on **how** they say these things. For example, you have noticed Rochester speaks in a rather strange way but not the way he seems to be ignoring the figure in front of him. You have sensed Jane's opposition but have **not developed** ideas about **how** she changes her way of addressing Rochester.

You have noticed that the use of **narrative voice** helps to shape and reinforce our response to Rochester's manner and ideas.

You have tried to focus on **particular words** (such as Rochester's use of beauty') and to bring together **words** and **phrases echoed** throughout the passage (such as Rochester's use of 'aerial', 'sylph' and 'angel').

You have not really explored the use of **narrative voice** in the extract but are aware of Jane's general opposition to Rochester's ideas.

You have used some examples of words and phrases to show clear differences in vocabulary and ways of speaking but **need to group** similar or contrasting echoes with appropriate comments in **more depth and consistency**.

Chapter 2 Prose non-fiction

Extracts from a Grade A answer

Scott seems self-restrained and even detached in his writing, as if he is trying to keep his emotions and fears under control. Even fear of injury is described in a measured way: 'Amputation is the least I can hope for now, but will the trouble spread?' There is a tone of factual resignation, an acceptance that things are not going to improve. This stoic attitude is expressed in phrases like 'I do not think we can hope for any better things now. We shall stick it out to the end'. There is a sense of quiet dignity in the face of massive odds. However, there are times when emotions can be glimpsed. There is a note of sarcasm when Scott writes 'What progress!' and a glimpse of passion and concern when he ends with 'For God's sake look after our people'.

In contrast, Byrd seems much more graphic and emotive in his writing. There is a feeling of energy and activity at the beginning in opposition to Scott's more passive acceptance. Byrd describes a 'black Friday' and how he 'awakened with a violent start'. He seems more angry and frustrated too and expresses this in his diary. He is not as resigned as Scott but almost bitter: I was Richard E. Byrd...and not worth a damn to myself or anybody else.' There is a greater sense of determination on his part, a will to survive: 'But you must have faith'. He seems to be willing to go through the mental battle Scott appears to have given up on; he admits that he has had 'melancholy thoughts' but that he did not have 'any feeling of resignation.' If anything his words convey his refusal to accept his potential fate in the way he 'rebelled' against the state of things. Byrd manages to sense a contrast in his way of life and to put matters into perspective; he does not seek help from God like Scott at the close of his diary but from his inner self. He realises that the 'homely, unpretentious things of life are the most important' and he realises how wrong his priorities have been.

Scott's language is matter-of-fact and unadorned by any poetic flourishes. It reflects the self-contained fortitude of his mood. He records things like the contents of their supper and the state of their location and the amount of supplies remaining: 'We are 15 miles from the depot and ought to get there in three days...We have two days' food but barely a day's fuel'. The diary records a gradual depletion of fuel and supplies ('no fuel and only one or two of food left') and the gathering of acceptance. The words reflect measured dignity about how to meet the end: 'Have decided it shall be natural – we shall march for the depot with or without our effects and die in our tracks... We shall stick it out to the end'. There is a bathetic note to the end of the diary; there is no outpouring or raging grief but a rather gentle note of regret, not so much about death but about the inability to go on recording things: 'It seems a pity, but I do not think I can write more'.

However, Byrd uses language in more forceful and powerful manner. His diary is marked by images of darkness to convey the depths of his dilemma. He has a 'black Friday'. He describes himself 'staring wildly into the darkness of the shack', aware of sensations and surroundings. The darkness is echoed later on when he personifies Death and his feelings towards it: 'But now death was a stranger sitting in a darkened room, secure in the knowledge that he would be there when I was gone.' He seems to feel submerged by the thoughts in his head; he feels himself 'sinking' and describes how 'Great waves of fear...swept through' him and 'settled deep within'. His battle seems to be internal and not the external world that Scott describes. Scott seems to record events outside while Byrd details the inner conflicts he faced. On the one hand he sees part of himself trapped and submerged by fear as the images of darkness and water suggest; but another part of him is free to reflect on things and this is expressed through images of flight: 'It is like a flight, a flight into another unknown. You start and you cannot turn back.'

Byrd writes in a much more dramatic and active style. We are plunged into his inner world and left in no doubt about his thoughts.

How to grade your answer

Grade A

You have explored the **mood** and **tone** in both passages and made a clear sense of **comparison**, noting the seeming resignation of the first extract and the more dynamic and passionate expression in the second.

You have explored the different **registers** in both extracts and the way the writer of the first passage seems resigned to his fate while the second wants to battle against it.

You have commented on the ways in which both writers **use language** to convey there ideas, sensing the rather more **detached style** of the first piece **compared** to the more **graphic** and **assertive** style of the second.

You have commented on the **use of contrast** in the second passage and explored how there seems to be a **tension** between the past and the present, between his current fears and his review of his life and the lessons he has learned.

You have commented on **patterns of imagery** in the second extract and sensed that there is some sort of **opposition** between them.

You have used **selective** and **brief quotations** effectively to offer **detailed** and discriminating **comparisons** between the two extracts.

Grade C

You have made some comments on the **mood** and **tone** but have not developed more detailed insights about the seeming resignation of the first extract and the more dynamic and passionate expression in the second.

You have shown some awareness of the different **registers** in the extracts but have not developed your comments to make full comparisons.

You have made some comments on the ways in which both writers use **language** to convey some of their **ideas**, but have not fully explored the **detached style** of the first piece compared to the more **graphic** one of the second.

You have made some comments on the **use of contrast** in the second passage but have not fully understood the **tension** between the past and present, between his fears and his review of his life and the lessons he has learned.

You have made few comments on the **patterns of imagery** in the second extract and have not really developed the idea of **opposition**.

You have made some effective use of **brief quotations** but could make more comments on the **qualities** they suggest and make **more comparative** points.

Chapter 3 Poetry

Extracts from a Grade A answer

The poem begins in a meditative and reminiscent mood as the poet contemplates the appearance of birch trees. There is a sense of a personal voice thinking of the present and the past. The ideas seem to progress in a meandering manner as certain words are repeated like building blocks, creating a process of memory and speculation. Words like 'swinging' and 'ice' help to achieve this effect. There is a sense of contrast not just between the past and present but in memories of the atmosphere and elements. The trees in the background are darker in contrast to the freedom suggested by the innocence of the boys swinging on the actual birches. This contrast is developed by the juxtaposition of ice with 'a sunny winter morning'. A feeling of restriction, of a lack of freedom within the natural world is conveyed by the manner in which the ice contains the branches. Slowly, the ice begins to melt and Frost employs some harsh sounds to suggest the liberation of the branches: 'cracks and crazes'. Light seems to bring a sense of relief but also a senses of some loss of rigid order: 'You'd think the inner dome of heaven had fallen'.

The introduction of 'heaven' suggests a more symbolic level to the poem now as the poet's voice grows more philosophical. The boughs are bent towards Earth, 'the right place , as Frost later comments, 'for love'; yet in his heart he longs to 'go by climbing a birch tree/And climb black branches up a snow-white trunk/Toward heaven'. The opposition of light and dark appears again here but now suggests that the real freedom for the poet is not that of the boys swinging on the birches on Earth as implied at the start of the poem but an ascent into the purity of heaven. He seems to have lost the urge to find innocent joy in this place as he grows older...

How to grade your answer

Grade A

You have described the **tone** and **mood** as well as commenting on the kind of voice used in the poem.

You have tried to use the sense of **contrast** to suggest possible ideas.

You have also explored the **use of contrast** in the **imagery** and have tried to see if any **patterns of imagery** shape the reader's response to the poem.

You have explored the **qualities** suggested by the **imagery**, again looking for possible **contrasts**.

You have considered the possible use of **motifs** or **symbols** in the imagery.

You have shown awareness of some some use of **syntax**.

You have commented on **differences** and **similarities** between **sections** of the poem in terms of **ideas**, **mood** and **patterns of imagery**.

You have considered some **other uses of language** such as the use of **sounds** by trying to suggest how they might reflect possible meaning.

Grade C

You have shown some awareness of **tone** and **mood** without quite developing comments on possible reasons why.

You have shown <u>some</u> sense of **contrast** without developing closer analysis.

You have implied that you are aware of **some aspects** of the **imagery** without quite sensing the nature of the contrasts.

You have commented on <u>some</u> of the qualities suggested by the **imagery**.

You have not really explored the possibilities of **symbols**.

You have shown limited awareness of the use of **syntax**.

You have shown some awareness of the **progression** of the poem without quite developing more detailed comments.

You have **identified** aspects such as the use of **sounds** without fully exploring how they might reflect possible meaning.

Chapter 4 Drama

Extracts from a Grade A answer

It seems that in this extract Vladimir is the leader, the one who asks the questions and gives the orders. Estragon seems more childlike and uncertain. The passage begins with Vladimir commanding his friend to 'Show your leg' and to 'Pull up your trousers'. The strange behaviour is undercut with humour in an almost farcical way as Estragon misunderstands the seriousness of Vladimir: 'Which?'. There is a slapstick element to the stage directions as Estragon stumbles about as Vladimir takes the leg. The audience are unsure whether it is the serious or humorous aspect they are meant to focus on. Vladimir becomes more insulting and commanding in his tone: 'The other, pig!' He sounds triumphant when he finds the object of his search, as if he has been proved right: 'There's the wound! Beginning to fester!'

There is a sense of triviality amidst all of his earnestness, an element of absurd over-concern in Vladimir's desire to be proved right. Yet there is also a sense of disorientation in the way Estragon seems unable to remember the most trivial of details, that is where he has misplaced his boots. For both tramps the topic takes on a level of serious importance and Vladimir's language becomes both dramatic and again triumphant as he solves the mystery. He must have an answer: 'No, I mean why did you throw them away… There they are… At the very spot where you left them yesterday.'

These concerns with memory and finding an answer mask the fact that they seem to be putting on an act; they cannot remember the real reason why they are here and the fact that the person they are waiting for has to give them an answer to something. They are only certain of one thing, and that thing is located in language. They cannot leave because they are 'waiting for Godot'. There is 'nothing' they can do about that fact. Instead they do something, rather than nothing, to occupy their time, using language and games to offer fulfilment. There is the focus on pointless questions and details such as the colour of the boots but beneath this the audience can, in Estragon's language, sense the deep seriousness and sense of futility in their wait. He, unlike the generally more rational Vladimir, expresses outbursts of emotion and frustration, each one playing off the other:

ESTRAGON: You see, all that's a lot of bloody –
VLADIMIR: Ah! I see what it is. Yes, I see what's happened.
ESTRAGON: All that's a lot of bloody –

Indeed, Estragon offers us glimpses of his despair: 'What'll we do, what'll we do!'

How to grade your answer

Grade A

You have sensed the use of **contrast** between the **characters** in terms of their **attitudes** and **outlooks**. You have understood that Vladimir gives the orders and seem intent on pursuing answers to minor questions when they lack an answer to why they are really there.

You have detected the sense of **hidden tension** and the fact that they seem to be putting on an **act** for some reason. You have noticed the ways in which questions and statements are used apparently to occupy the time.

You have shown an appreciation of the mixture of **moods** in the passage, the blend of the trivial and serious, the absurd and real pain.

You have shown a grasp of the **progression** of the passage and the **differences** between sections. You have sensed, for example, the blend of the comic and the earnest at the beginning and the real sense of frustration in Estragon at the close.

You have explored the **use of language** of both characters, the ways in which they address each other, the ways in which **control of the dialogue** is established. For example, you have commented on Vladimir's use of orders and particular questions.

Grade C

You have sensed <u>some</u> elements of **contrast** between the **characters** in terms of their **attitudes** and **outlooks**. You have implied that Vladimir seems to be in charge without fully developing ideas about how he does this through his use of language.

You have offered some comments on the fact that there appears to be an **underlying tension**. You are not so sure what the underlying tension is nor have you fully explored the ways in which the tramps seem to be passing time.

You have shown <u>some</u> appreciation of the **moods** in the passage without developing closer comments on the mixture or the range.

You have shown <u>some</u> competent understanding of the **progression** of the passage without fully exploring the **differences** between them.

You have made some comments on the **use of language** but have not used **brief quotations** as much as you could to explore the ideas behind them and what they tell us about the speakers.

Chapter 5 Speech and dialogue

Extracts from a Grade A answer

The speaker in passage A addresses her audience in a very informal manner, seeking to create a personal and relaxed atmosphere: 'call me Ame...everybody else do'. The use of phatic language and fillers also adds to this feeling of informality: for example, the speaker says 'well for a start...and our dad said to I well he said'. The use of hesitation and repetition shows the speaker recalling and thinking. We can sense this spontaneous speech not only by the pauses but by the changing directions in topic and ideas in the first paragraph. The speaker's regional manner of speech can be located in her vocabulary such as 'seed' and 'carns't'; there is deviation from standard speech in the way the past tense has been created and dialect variations on 'can't'. These words also imply that the pronunciation has a particular accent where vowel sounds are drawn out in quite an emphatic manner. The speaker's grammar adds to this nature of informal recollection; words are used in an 'incorrect' way ('everybody else do') or agreement is inappropriate ('they was paying'). The character seems to have roots in the place where she was brought up and has retained some of the more archaic words from the area: 'he said if thee'. This combination of grammar and vocabulary gives the impression of the speaker's sense of tradition and awareness of the past.

Passage B also tries to convey a sense of tradition and a regional way of life but in a much more constructed manner. There is less use of fillers but Hardy does try to convey the idea of emphatic phrasing when italics are used in Mrs Dewy's words 'as in them'. Mrs Dewy is given the attributes of a regional dialect through her use of words like ''til' and ''tis' and the use of inappropriate grammar: 'there be you'. This creates the sense of an informal discussion, a sense of banter in the way she addresses her husband. She is given her own particular vocabulary, indicating a domestic and down to earth view of life, keen to save money and distrustful of other people: 'that will make an honest waistcoat; all by my contriving in buying the stuff at a bargain and having it made up under my eye... and not going straight to the rascally tailors'. She also uses down to earth idioms like 'Lord-a mercy', again implying a down to earth everyday outlook. Perhaps, though, unlike a spontaneous speech her words also contain figurative language ('as fat as a porpoise') which may seem more literary and out of context. She is by far the dominant speaker and her outpouring represents her energy and endeavours to be busy and effective.

In the same way Reuben is also given the attributes of a regional dialect in the way he speaks: ''Tis my warm nater in summer-time, I suppose. I always did get in such a heat when I bustle about.' The phonetic spelling of 'nater' is intended to indicate the nature of his accent; the use of ''Tis' echoes the linguistic contractions that his wife uses and adds to the informal atmosphere; his vocabulary seems to use place-specific expressions so that 'summer' becomes 'summer-time'; he uses idioms like 'in such a heat' instead of the more direct 'get hot'. He employs verbs which initially suggest energy and effort ('bustle') but which turn into images of mild activity when the word 'about' is tagged on the end. The phrases conveys the rather diffident and idle nature that his wife complains that he has.

Beyond the two contrasting speakers there is a third voice – that of the author. Hardy's comments highlight the humorous contrast between the husband and wife: 'with the severity justifiable in a long-tried companion' directs the reader's attention to the fact that although she seems to be pushing her husband rather hard, she is, in fact, the one who has been put upon most over the years...

How to grade your answer

Grade A

You have shown a clear sense of **audience**, **purpose** and **context** in commenting on the transcript of natural speech.

You have shown **awareness** of the effect of fillers and pauses.

You have commented on the speaker's **vocabulary**, **pronunciation** and **grammar** and considered the effects they create.

You have considered the ways in which fictional dialogue tries to **construct** the rhythms of spontaneous speech.

You have explored the ways in which the fictional speakers use **vocabulary** and **grammar** and discussed the **impressions** they create.

You have shown a discriminating awareness of the contrasts between the speakers and explored how these contrasts are evoked in the way they speak and the language they use.

Grade C

You have shown <u>some</u> awareness of **audience**, **purpose** and **context** in commenting on the transcript.

You have **identified** rather than commented on the use of fillers and pauses.

You have **identified** features of **vocabulary**, **pronunciation** and **grammar** but offered limited comments on them.

You have explored <u>some</u> of the ways in which fictional dialogue tries to seem like natural speech.

You have explored <u>some</u> of the ways in which fictional speakers use vocabulary and grammar.

You have shown <u>some awareness</u> of the contrasts between the speakers but have not fully explored how and why they are established.

You have shown an awareness of the ways in which **authorial voice** can be used in fictional dialogue to shape the reader's responses and to help create mood.

You have shown <u>limited awareness</u> of the ways in which the authorial voice can be used in fictional dialogue to shape the reader's responses.

Chapter 6 Directed writing

Extracts from a Grade A answer

(a)   New York. The place to get around in. Famous for its yellow cabs. But have you thought about using the subway?

It's fast and it's cheap. And it gives you freedom to travel when and where you want.

New Yorkers themselves know this. That's why over a million people a day use it.

Offering easy access and links to local connecting buses, the subway is easy to step into and step off.

The stations are light and airy, decorated in a modern and hi-tech style. We have recently finished a massive refurbishment programme, improving security features and decor to make your journeys all the more relaxing and enjoyable.

And it couldn't be easier to use.

There are easy to read directions and people are always on hand to help out if you are not sure…

(b)   The original extract presents a very dark and hostile place. The writer makes the subway resemble some sort of gothic prison with references to 'bars..and steel gates'; it sounds the kind of place no one returns from. In my creative piece I tried to convey a sense of freedom and lightness by using phrases like 'light and airy'; the original extract suggests that the subway is full of trouble and creates all kinds of difficulty – in fact it is 'easy to get lost' while I suggest that it is 'easy' to use. I have tried to highlight the practicality of travelling in this way.

The extract is written in an assertive and negative style. The writer voices opinions in a direct and unqualified way: 'The subway is frightening'and piles on lists of words to reinforce this negative image, almost trying to find the precise expression needed: It is 'sometimes not pity, but fear; bewilderment, curiosity'. There is an impersonal tone to the passage with the visitor seen as outsider, a 'stranger' who does not share the knowledge or experience of New Yorkers. In my piece I have tried to make the potential visitor feel welcome, highlighting how easy the subway is to use and writing in a reassuring style, implying 'people' (without openly suggesting New Yorkers) are always there to help.

I feel that I have managed to offer an alternative approach to the original extract by using words and phrases that suggest qualities of freedom and light as opposed to entrapment and darkness. However I am not sure that the opening to the piece is suitable enough for a script. Maybe it seems too abrupt and lacking in focus; there is no real hook or sense that this is aimed initially at visitors to the city…

How to grade your answer

Part (a)

Grade A

You have clearly sensed the **purpose** of the script – that it is there to persuade people.

You have **not** included negative ideas from the original piece.

Grade C

You have <u>some</u> sense of the **purpose** of the script but have not fully recognised that this is the opening and must engage the viewers at once.

You have included some negative ideas from the original piece.

You have promoted the decorative features of the subway in a **positive** light – its possible historic or hi-tech appearance, its decoration, its sense of security and strength.

You have suggested that New York people regard the subway as one of the city's strengths and an effective means of transport.

You might also suggest that New Yorkers use the subway regularly, are helpful guides and that finding your way round is easy and directions are clear.

You have mentioned some of the decorative features of the subway and/or its security.

You have made some reference to New Yorkers but **not highlighted** how highly they regard the subway.

You have made some reference to the helpfulness of New Yorkers without fully highlighting how helpful they always are.

Part (b)

Grade A

Your commentary uses quotations from both the original extract and your own writing. You may have noted the personal mode of address of the original, its negativity, its use of imagery to suggest prison, its attempts to explain by using several related words ('pity… fear… bewilderment… curiosity'), its use of strong assertive phrases ('Verbal directions are incomprehensible…'), the impersonal use of New Yorkers and the 'stranger'.

Your own writing has positive and uplifting words. You are aware of some of the more successful and less successful features of your own writing.

Grade C

Your commentary makes some use of quotations but tends to focus on some of the surface features such as the use of repetitive structures.

You have not fully engaged with the writer's use of imagery and the qualities it suggests. You may be aware that you have retained some of the negative features of the original in your own writing.

You have not really addressed the strengths and limitations of your own writing.

Chapter 7 Further exam questions

Prose fiction and non-fiction

How to grade your answer

Grade A

You have explored in detail the **use of voice** in both passages, realising how the **first person voice** in the first passage contributes a sense of immediacy, inner reflection and physicality in the non-literary piece, while the **authorial voice** in the fictional second passage focuses more on the action and tension of the surroundings.

You have commented on how the **settings** suggest enclosure in both passages; the unpleasant conditions in the first passage are matched by the dark and rainy conditions of the second. Both settings inflict physical and mental pain and disorientation on the **characters**.

You have noted how the first passage conveys a sense of active movement in its **vocabulary and expression** moving towards a sense of liberation and celebration; while the second passage also suggests action, tension (with words which suggest movement and then inaction) and silence in the darkness, with its use of **brief dialogue** and **images** of darkness which give way to scenes of light and dramatic confusion.

Grade C

You have made some relevant and informed comments about the **use of voice** in both passages, realising that we seem to be with the narrator herself in the first extract and that the second passage seems to focus more on the **setting** and **tension**.

You have made some good comments on the **use of setting** in both extracts without probing deeply enough the ways in which it adds to the tension itself by referring to specific aspects of the conditions and moods created.

You have made some reasonable comments on the use of **vocabulary** and **expression** in the first passage without fully exploring the progression from the initial mood to the one of liberation at the end; you have understood some aspects of the **images** of darkness in the second passage without developing the **patterns of images** further.

You have explored some of the uses of **syntax** in the first passage, noting perhaps the use of direct and brief sentences to convey urgency; and its use in the second passage in terms of alternating lengthy sentences punctuated by briefer ones to convey the sense of stopping and starting in the escape itself.

You have not really explored the use of **syntax** in both extracts.

Poetry

Question 1 How to grade your answer

Grade A

You have commented on the almost romantic and nostalgic **tone** of Poem A with its sense of triumph and certainty, and its patriotic feel compared to the more stark and realistic picture conveyed by Poem B.

You have also noticed how the **voice** in Poem B moves from an almost cold feeling at the start to a degree of pity and understanding for the enemy.

You have commented on the ways in which Poem A focuses on the poet himself while the second moves towards an understanding of wider issues and a degree of reconciliation with the enemy.

You have commented on the use of nature **imagery** in Poem A and the idea of a life–death cycle.

You have noticed the use of **syntax** in Poem A where the use of careful repetition creates a seemingly calm and rational mood. In Poem B, by contrast, the imagery is stark and unpleasant, hard and physical.

You have sensed that the **syntax** in Poem B creates an awkward and jolting effect with its use of internal and half rhyme, repeated phrases, and key placed words like 'overshadowing'.

You have commented on the use and effect of the **sonnet** form in Poem A compared to the seemingly awkward style of Poem B.

Grade C

You have shown some awareness of the **tone** of Poem A without probing its nostalgic and romantic feel in depth. You have shown an awareness of the more brutal **tone** of Poem B without fully comparing both texts

You have offered some comment on the ending of Poem B without fully exploring its significance in comparison to the opening.

You have shown some awareness of the focus of Poem A but have not really explored the ways in which Poem B seems to move to a wider sense of understanding.

You have made some comments on the use of nature **imagery** in Poem A without fully exploring the patterns of words.

You have made some brief or passing comments on the use of **syntax** in Poem A without commenting on its contribution to the mood. You are aware of the stark **imagery** in Poem B.

You have made some comments on the use of **syntax** in Poem B without fully exploring the use of **rhyme** and **sounds**.

You have identified the **sonnet** form in Poem A without really commenting on its use and have made limited comparisons to the form of Poem B.

Question 2 How to grade your answer

Grade A

You have commented on the **use of voice** in the poem, its sense of honesty and regret and how it contributes to a sense of increasing despair.

You have noted that the **voice** is a painfully honest one, aware of time passing, missed opportunities and futile efforts to capture meaning and emotions.

You have explored the way the narrator is caught between two worlds, the mundane process of shopping and the continual inner voice going on as she carries out this task. You have commented on the way these **contrasts** come together at the close as the narrator sees herself in a mirror.

Grade C

You have made some comments on the **use of voice** in the poem without quite noticing the increasing sense of despair as the poem progresses.

You have noticed that the voice is open and honest without commenting fully on the increasing sense of futility.

You have sensed that the narrator is caught between two worlds but have not explored the effects that this **contrast** has on our understanding of the narrator.

You have explored the different **tones** of these past and present worlds, the sense of hope compared to the boredom and despair of the present.

You have commented on the use of **brief phrases** as she goes through the motions of shopping, the sense of **direct self-examination** and **recognition of moods** and of her life as suggested by the title.

You have made some comments on the use of **tone** but have not fully commented on their nature

You have shown a partial awareness of the use of **syntax** and **phrasing** without fully commenting on how they shape our interpretation of the narrator.

Drama

Question 1 How to grade your answer

Grade A

You have commented in detail on the ways in which Lady Macbeth attempts to **control** her husband through a mixture of flattery and commands.

You have explored in detail the **contrasting attitudes** each character displays to the course of events: her more focused and practical awareness compared to his inward-looking thoughts and feelings.

You have examined the ways in which Lady Macbeth becomes less scared as the scene **develops** and the ways in which her husband seems to grow more distant and cut-off from immediate reality

You have commented in detail on Lady Macbeth's rather abrupt and dismissive comments, as if the guilt can be instantly erased compared to Macbeth's haunted mind and lingering sense of fear.

You have examined the **use of language and imagery**, noting, for example how Lady Macbeth sees water as ordinary while to Macbeth it carries symbolic connotations.

Grade C

You have made some competent comments on the ways in which Lady Macbeth tries to **control** her husband without quite understanding the full range of methods she uses.

You have made some relevant points about the **contrasting attitudes** of each character but have not fully developed your comments.

You have examined some of the ways in which each character **develops** as the scene progresses but have not commented on how they appear to be more disunited rather than united at this point in their joint venture.

You have made some effective points about the differences between the characters' comments without developing them in detail.

You have made some good comments on the characters' **use of language** but have not probed the use of **imagery** and its **symbolic connotations**.

Question 2 How to grade your answer

Grade A

You have sensed the changing nature of **control** as the scene develops. Sylvia seems to be the senior figure in the first half but Paul gradually asserts his sense of status.

You have explored how the **stage directions** at the start convey Sylvia's need to put on act to seem as if she is in charge and in control of the office. She is also concerned that her appearance is correct. You have realised that towards the end of the scene the stage directions reveal her starting the work for Paul as she uncovers the typewriter and opens the directory for him.

You have commented on the ways in which the characters **speak to each other** in rather formal and polite **tones** but soon begin offering informal and personal confidences to each other.

You have noted the **development** of each character, Paul becoming increasingly assertive and Sylvia seemingly offering supportive comments to allow the conversation to unfold.

Grade C

You have sensed some of the aspects of **control** in the extract without quite exploring how they unfold in clear stages.

You have made some competent comments on the use of **stage directions** while not quite detecting how they contribute fully to the understanding of the **situation** and **characters**.

You have made some comments on the ways in which the characters **speak to each other** without quite exploring the switch from formality to personal confidences in close depth.

You have offered a clear sense of how each character **develops** in the scene without fully understanding Sylvia's contribution, her wish to be second fiddle in the office and in the conversation.

You have explored the absence of **imagery** in the extract and the ways in which the language seems **prosaic** and even **clichéd** in order to convey the ordinariness of the characters' lives at this point.

You have sensed the lack of **imagery** in the passage but have not really explored the **language** beyond this.

Speech and dialogue

Question 1 How to grade your answer

Grade A

You have explored the ways in which the speaker seems to talk in an honest manner but actually **evades** confronting the real issues and have successfully included that in your own writing.

You have commented on how the speaker **blends** a sense of personal commitment with a strong sense of sentimentality, patriotism and even religion. You have successfully **reflected** this mixture in your own writing.

You have commented on the personal **mode of address** and the apparent **trust** the speaker seeks to establish, as well as his **pledges** and **promises**, a technique you have captured in your creative piece.

You have commented on the use of **abstract nouns** and the use of **rhetorical devices** such as lists of three and the use of particular **strong terms** ('purged', ugly mob violence') combined with those of **pathos** and sentimentality ('I love America...I deeply believe) and have sought to use this in your own piece.

Grade C

You have noted the rather **evasive tone** of the speaker and have captured this in your own writing to a degree.

You have shown some awareness of how the speaker **blends** different styles of **register** without quite probing its effect further. You have captured this blend to some effect in your own writing.

You have commented on the personal **mode of address** and offered some competent awareness of the speaker's attempts to sound honest and open.

You have made some good comments on the speaker's use of **rhetorical devices** without describing their effects as much as you could have done. Some of them may be identified rather than commented on. You have captured some of these devices in your own creative piece.

Question 2 How to grade your answer

Grade A

You have commented in detail on how the author creates a sense of **dialect** and **accent** through the use of **phonetic spelling** (such as 'pecooliar' and 'partickler'), non-standard **grammar** (for example, 'in comparison with which young man I am a Angel'), the selection of certain words and phrases to indicate a particular **place or region** (such as 'vittles').

You have commented in detail on the use of **syntax** in the passage and the way in which the criminal speaks in rather elongated sentences, hardly seeming to pause for breath.

You have explored the use of the narrator's use of **Standard English** with its more formal and correct **tone** and recognisable **vocabulary**.

You have considered the ways in which these **contrasts** in the speech of the narrator and criminal convey different **tones** and **attitudes** and commented on them in detail.

Grade C

You have made some competent comments on the ways in which the author has attempted to create a sense of **dialect and accent** but may have tended to identify these techniques rather than commenting on their effects in the passage.

You have made some reference to the use of **syntax** without quite developing closer comments on the effect of it.

You have made some reference to the narrator's use of **language** without specifying in detail its exact nature and construction.

You have shown some awareness of a basic **contrast** between the narrator and the criminal but have not fully explored how **tone** and **attitudes** differ and the effect this has on our response to the passage.

Directed writing

Question 1 How to grade your answer

Grade A

You have clearly identified the **audience** for the advertisement as one interested in style and decor. Presumably they are concerned with modern design and possibly owning their own property and have money to spend.

You have commented on the **mode of address** and the informal and personal style of the text and reflected this in your own piece of creative writing.

You have also included the sense of lifestyle and **aspiration** in your own advertisement and have commented on the way in which the original tries to dress up a rather mundane product in **descriptive** and flowery tones.

You have explored the way that the original advertisement employs artistic **imagery** and the use of modern or seemingly **technical** words (like 'gleaming chrome', 'makeover', 'high-efficiency') and have incorporated these into your own creative piece.

You have considered the use of **syntax** and the use of **questions**; you have noted the use of words which suggest flattery, opportunity and ease ('perfect system...minimum of fuss' for example).

Grade C

You have made some sound comments on the nature of the **audience** without quite probing how this has shaped choices of vocabulary in the original text and in your own writing.

You have sensed the relaxed nature of the **mode of address** and included this in your own writing through the use of words like 'you'.

You have shown some awareness of the use of **lifestyle** in the original and made a competent attempt to reflect this in your own writing.

You have made some comments on the use of **colour** in the original advertisement but have not really commented on the patterns of words concerning art nor how they are combined with technical words to convey a sense of style and design.

You have made only limited references to the use of **syntax** but have sensed the use of **questions** to create an informal and personal tone.

Question 2 How to grade your answer

Grade A

You have commented on the nature of the **audience** as one with a possible sense of style and taste – one which the advertiser feels likes luxury and refinement.

You have used **brief quotations** to explore how the text seeks to **flatter** and offer the potential customer choice and luxury. The informal and personal **mode of address** has also been included in your own creative writing.

You have considered the use of **adjectives** and **superlatives** which offer reassurance, choice and a sense of the customer being both in control and pampered by the company. You have successfully **reflected** these processes in your own advertisement.

You have noted how the original piece attempts to make all aspects of the journey sound relaxing and evocative of both the **modern** and the **traditional**. You have sought to capture these aspects.

You have commented on the use of **atmospheric** words like 'baguette' and 'ambience' which try to convey a French flavour and have tried to incorporate a similar technique in your advertisement.

Grade C

You have made a sound attempt to comment on the nature of the **audience** without fully saying how it affects the choice of language.

You have shown some awareness of how the original advertisement tries to make the customer feel at ease and have included the personal **mode of address** in your own creative writing.

You have shown a degree of understanding of the ways in which some **descriptive terms** have been used to create a sense of luxury. You have made a sound attempt to **reflect** some of this process in your own writing.

You have made partial comments on how the original advertisement tries to use a blend of the **modern** or **traditional** but have not really followed this through in your own creative writing.

You have not really detected the use of **atmospheric** French terms in your commentary nor in your own creative response.